Contents

KU-520-228

What is spring?

There are four seasons — spring, summer, autumn and winter. In spring the air begins to get warmer after the cold days of winter. Spring is not the same everywhere. In some countries spring can last for two or three months. In countries near the middle part of the world spring can be a very short season.

What signs of spring can you see in this picture?

Here are two signs that spring has come.
■ New green leaves start to grow on the trees.
■ It is light early in the morning, and still light in the evening.
Can you think of any more?

In many parts of the world the beginning of spring is a time to celebrate. Some celebrations are very old. Can you think of any holidays during the spring?

PROJECT: Make a 'pop-up' card

You can make your own 'pop-up' card to celebrate spring.

You will need
- Thin card 21cm x 30cm (8in x 12in)
- Felt-tip pens
- Scissors

What to do

1. Fold the card in half. Fold down the top corner on the folded edge.

2. Open out the card, then close it again, tucking the folded corner inside.

3. Cut off the top. Open the card. You will see the middle piece pop up.

4. Cut the middle piece into the shape of a spring flower and colour it in.

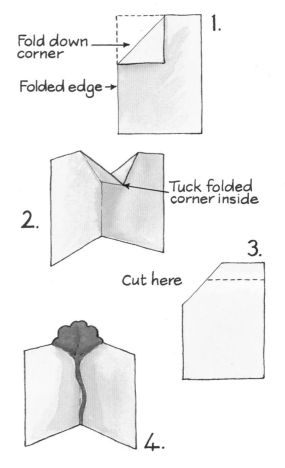

Fold down corner

Folded edge →

1.

Tuck folded corner inside

2.

Cut here

3.

4.

Clouds and rain

Spring is often a season of damp and cloudy weather. Clouds are made of tiny droplets of water. You can make a cloud in a bottle.

PROJECT: Make a cloud

ASK AN ADULT TO HELP WITH THIS EXPERIMENT.

You will need
- A large plastic bottle, with the cap still on
- A sharp knife
- Warm water
- Ice cubes
- A table lamp or a sunny window-sill

What to do

1. Carefully cut the top third off the bottle.

2. Put some warm water into the bottom part. Put some ice cubes into the top part.

3. Put the top part, upside down, into the bottom part.

4. Place the bottle on a sunny window-sill, or near a table lamp. Watch to see how the cloud forms in the bottom part.

Spring weather can also be very changeable. Some days are warm and sunny, others quite chilly. There may be a lot of rain, very little or none at all. The wind might be gentle and warm, or strong and cold.

Over the next few pages you will find out how to keep a record of all these changes.

Take your measurements at the same time every day. Record them on a chart like this one.

Date	Rainfall in mm	Temperature in °C	Wind speed (number of times marked cup went round in 1 minute)	Wind direction
26 April	3mm	14°	30	from the west

PROJECT: Make a rain gauge

ASK AN ADULT TO HELP WITH THIS EXPERIMENT.

You will need
- A large plastic bottle with a flat bottom. Take the cap off.
- A sharp knife
- A ruler
- Four bricks

What to do

1. Carefully cut the top third off the bottle.

2. Place the bottom part out in the open. Surround it with the four bricks so it won't blow away.

3. Put the top part into the bottom, upside down.

4. Leave it to catch the rain.

5. Measure the amount of rain in the bottle with the ruler. If the bottle is empty, record '0' on your chart.

6. Empty the bottle after taking each measurement.

Warmth and wind

As spring goes on, the **temperature** usually gets warmer and warmer, but sometimes there may be a cold spell. You can measure the temperature as part of your weather records.

PROJECT: Recording the temperature

You will need
- An outdoor thermometer
- A light coloured washing-up liquid bottle with the top and bottom cut off
- Masking tape
- A fence post somewhere out of the wind and direct sunlight

What to do

1. Tape your bottle to the top of the fence post.

2. Slide your thermometer into the bottle. Check it every day and record the temperature.

PROJECT: Make an anemometer

Sometimes temperature depends on the strength and direction of the wind. You can measure wind strength with an anemometer.

You will need
- A washing-up liquid bottle
- Five thin wooden dowels, one 30cm (12in) long and four 20cm (8in) long
- A large cork
- Four plastic cups, one marked with coloured tape
- Clear sticky tape
- A sharp knife

What to do

1. Cut a hole in the bottom of the washing-up liquid bottle. Cut the nozzle off the cap.

2. Sharpen one end of the long dowel and push it into the bottom of the cork.

3. Sharpen one end of each short dowel and push it into the side of the cork. Push the other end through a plastic cup. Stick with clear tape.

4. Put the long dowel through the plastic bottle.

5. Hold the bottle in the wind. Count how many times the marked cup blows round in one minute.

Is it colder or warmer on the windiest days?

ASK AN ADULT TO HELP
WITH THIS EXPERIMENT.

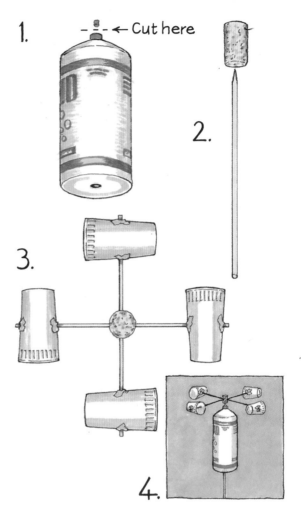

1. ← Cut here

2.

3.

4.

Wind direction

A wind vane tells you the direction of the wind. Winds may be warm or cold depending on where they come from. Where does your warmest wind come from? Where does your coldest wind come from? Winds are named after the the direction from which they blow.

PROJECT: Make a wind vane

You will need
- Two plastic straws
- Two nails
- Sticky tape
- A piece of card, 12cm x 8cm (5in x 3in)
- A cork tile
- A compass
- Scissors
- Two bricks

What to do

1. Cut a triangle out of one end of the card. Make all three sides the same length.

2. Stick the triangle to one end of a straw. Stick the rest of the card to the other end.

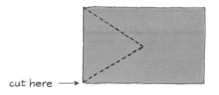

cut here →

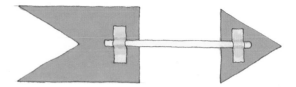

3. Push a nail through the middle of the straw.

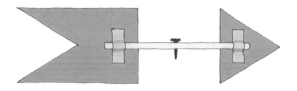

4. Mark North (N), South (S), East (E) and West (W) on the cork tile. Push your other nail through the middle of the cork tile from underneath.

5. Slide your second straw over the nail in the cork tile. Slide the nail through the pointer straw into the other end of the second straw.

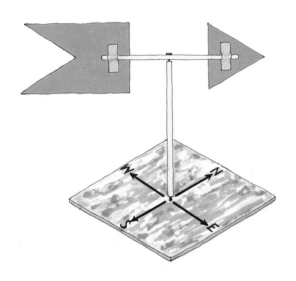

6. Take your wind vane outside. Use your compass to make sure the marks on the stand are pointing the right way. Use bricks to hold the cork tile down. The arrow will point into the direction the wind is coming from.

7. Record wind direction every day for a month.

Which way does the wind most often blow from? This is called the prevailing wind.

Fly a kite

Spring is a good time for flying kites. Kites can be made in many shapes and sizes. The biggest ones can lift an adult.

Even this colourful 'caterpillar' kite can fly.

PROJECT: Make a kite

You will need
- A plastic rubbish sack
- Two thin garden canes
- Strong sticky tape
- String wound around a short, smooth stick
- Scissors
- A small saw
- A tape measure or ruler

What to do

1. Cut open the sack and spread it out. Cut the canes to fit the short side of the cut sack. Stick them on to the sack like this.

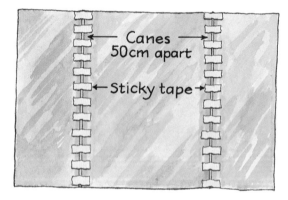

Canes
50cm apart

Sticky tape

2. Cut the sides of the kite into a shape like this:

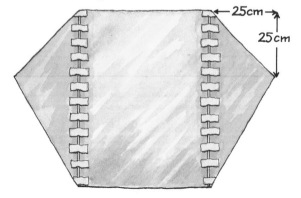

25cm

25cm

14

3. Cut a 4m (12ft) length of string. Tie a knot at each end and stick firmly on to the inside of each side of the kite. This is called the bridle.

How to fly your kite

1. Tie the kite string very firmly on to the middle of the bridle.

2. Let out about 40m (120ft) of string.

3. Stand with your back to the wind.

4. Ask a friend to hold the kite as high as they can and to let it go when the wind fills it.

5. Let out the string as quickly as you can. If the kite begins to fall, give the string a gentle tug to make it rise again.

To make your kite **aerobatic**, tie two strings to it instead of a bridle. Hold each string, again wound round short, smooth sticks, in a different hand. Wear gloves. To make your kite dive and loop you pull the two strings at different times.

Building homes

Birds build nests in spring so they can lay their eggs. Birds often make very beautiful nests. They use many kinds of materials. Some weave stalks of grass and other plants. Some coat their nests with mud to make them stronger.

PROJECT: Build a nest

What to do

Collect some materials that you think would make a strong nest. Try dried grass, moss, hair and mud. See if you can make them into a nest. Are you as clever with your hands, as the bird is with its beak?

It is important that you never interfere with a nest that has eggs or baby birds in it. You may frighten the parents away for ever. Old nests are often full of insects and other small animals that may be harmful.

PROJECT: Testing bricks

It is not only birds that use mud for building. In many parts of the world people make bricks from mud to build houses. You can test the strength of different kinds of mud bricks.

You will need
- Mud
- Sand
- Gravel
- Straw
- A long cardboard tube
- A metal weight or large marble
- Small soft cheese cartons, or tin foil trays

What to do

1. Divide your mud into four piles.

2. Add some sand to one pile, some gravel to another and some straw to a third. Leave the last pile pure mud.

3. Make some mud bricks from each pile, using the cartons or trays as a mould. Let the bricks dry thoroughly.

4. Put the tube on to each of the bricks. Drop the weight or marble down the tube.

Does the brick break? Are there any marks on the brick? Why is it important for the weight to be dropped from the same height?

Frogs and tadpoles

Frogs lay their eggs in the early spring. The eggs of a frog are called spawn. They usually take about two weeks to hatch.

The frog in this picture is laying its spawn in a pond.

The little animals that hatch out are called tadpoles. At first they breathe through **gills** on the outside of their bodies. As the tadpoles grow bigger, skin grows over their gills and hides them. In time, their back legs begin to grow, followed by the front ones. Their **lungs** soon start to develop, and they begin to turn into frogs.

When tadpoles first hatch they eat small water plants. As they grow bigger they eat small animals that live in the water.

If you keep tadpoles at home or at school, you must make sure that they have the right food. Use clean water from the pond where you got your frog spawn, not tap water. Put in a large stone or brick for the growing frogs to rest on out of the water.

These tadpoles are feeding on a dead stickleback.

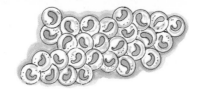

PROJECT: Draw a life cycle chart

You can make a chart to show the **life cycle** of a frog.

```
You will need
• Card
• Paper fastener (split pin)
• Coloured pencils or pens
• Scissors
```

What to do

1. Draw the stages of the life cycle of a frog like this.

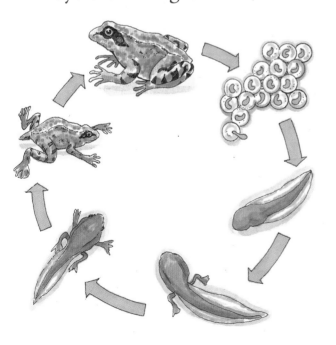

2. Cut out a pointer from the card. Fix it to the middle of your drawing with the paper fastener.

3. Watch your tadpoles change. Put the dates of the changes on your drawing.

4. Measure how long it takes to change from one stage to another.

How long does it take for the frog spawn to become frogs?

It is very important to return the tadpoles to the pond when they have changed into frogs. Do not try to keep them as pets.

Spring flowers

Look carefully at a flower. You will see that it is made up of several different parts. Look inside the petals. Can you find the things in this picture?

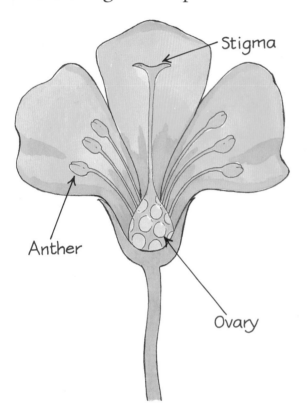

Stigma

Anther

Ovary

The stigma is the part the pollen settles on. Pollen can be carried to the stigma by insects or other small animals, or be blown by the wind.

The ovary is where the seeds are made. In many plants this becomes a fruit which has seeds inside.

The anther carries the pollen. Pollen is like yellow dust. Look at some through a strong magnifying glass. What shapes are the grains of pollen? The pollen often has to move from one plant to another to make seeds.

In spring the air is full of pollen. It can make you sneeze and make your eyes sore. This is called hay fever, because a lot of the pollen comes from grass.

PROJECT: Make a pollen trap

You can make a pollen trap that catches pollen in the air.

What to do

1. Cut a square hole out of each piece of card to make a frame.

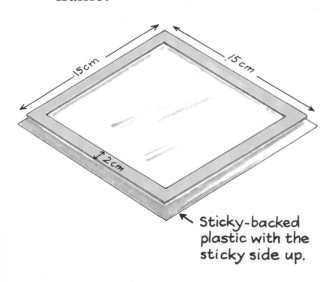

15cm · 15cm · 2cm

Sticky-backed plastic with the sticky side up.

2. Place the frames on the sticky side of the plastic. Cut off any spare plastic.

3. Leave at least six traps with the sticky side up around the garden or school grounds for a few days.

4. Look at them through a magnifying glass.

Can you see any pollen? Are all the grains the same shape? How much of the plastic is covered? Is there any dirt on the plastic?

Growing seeds

Many seeds **germinate** in spring. Seeds are often sown indoors in boxes before being planted out.

Above: Seeds sown in boxes in a greenhouse get an early start.

PROJECT: A soil experiment

You will need
- Plastic seed boxes
- Clean soil
- Dry sand
- Seeds

What to do

1. Fill one box with sand, and one with soil.

2. Make up different mixtures of soil and sand and fill your other boxes.

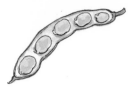

3. Label each one so you know which mixture is in which box.

4. Plant some seeds in each box. Cover them with the sand, soil, or the sand and soil mixture.

5. Water the seeds. Place the boxes in a warm, airy place.

6. Record when the seeds begin to grow.

Let them grow for a while to see if they prefer a particular mix of soil. Do the seeds grow well in sand?

PROJECT: Watching seeds grow

You will need
- A large plastic bottle
- Blotting paper
- Water
- A broad bean and a maize (corn-on-the-cob) seed

What to do

1. Cut the top off the plastic bottle. Put the blotting paper round the inside of the bottle.

2. Put the seeds down between the bottle and the paper.

4. Put a little water in the bottle.

5. Record what you see happening to your seeds. How long does it take for something to happen? Does the root or the stem grow first? Do they look the same for each seed?

The greenhouse

Many plants need protection from the weather in the early part of the year. A good start means they will have better fruit and flowers later on.

A greenhouse will give them warm, wet air in which to grow. The sun can shine through the glass and the air will become warm. When the plants are watered, some of the water will stay inside the greenhouse because the glass will not let it escape.

This gardener is growing plants in his greenhouse. They would die if he put them outdoors in cold weather.

PROJECT: Make a mini-greenhouse

You will need
- A large seed tray
- Four garden canes 30cm (12in) long
- Two canes a bit longer than the long side of the tray, and two a bit longer than the short side
- Sticky tape or pipe cleaners
- Clear plastic sheet
- Gravel or sand

What to do

1. Stand a 30cm cane upright in each corner of the tray. Fill the tray with sand or gravel to hold the canes in place.

2. Fix the other canes to the top of the upright canes with sticky tape or pipe cleaners.

3. Cover the canes with the plastic sheet. Make small openings in the sides for air to get in and out.

4. Stand pot plants in the tray. Water them regularly.

The air that surrounds the earth can act like a gigantic greenhouse. Sunlight reaches the earth by passing through the air, just as it passes through the glass of a greenhouse. As the earth gets warm, part of the air, called carbon dioxide, traps this heat and won't let it escape. This is called the greenhouse effect. We make carbon dioxide every time we burn fuel, and we breathe it out from our bodies. More and more carbon dioxide is being made every year. The sea can **absorb** a lot of it from the air, and plants need it to live. This is why it is very important to keep the sea clean, and not to cut down the forests.

What could happen to the ice at the **North** and **South Poles** if the air gets warmer?

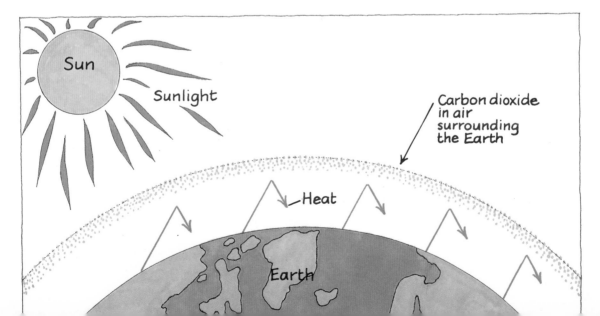

Levers

Preparing the garden for young plants in spring can be heavy work. A lever is a simple machine that makes lifting weights easier. There are three types of lever. We use all of them in the garden.

Using a spade is an example of a first type lever. The balancing point or pivot is between the effort which is at one end, and the load which is at at the other end. Most levers are this type because it is the best for lifting weights more easily.

A wheelbarrow is a second type lever. The pivot is at one end, the load is in the middle, and the effort is at the other end.

A third type lever has the load at one end, the pivot at the other, and the effort in the middle. Our arms can be this type of lever. It is not so easy to lift heavy weights with a third type as with a first or second type lever.

You can make models of all these levers.

PROJECT: Making levers

You will need
- Card
- Paper fasteners (split pins)
- Scissors

What to do

1. Use a large sheet of card for the backing.

2. Cut out several strips of card for the levers.

3. Fix the strips of card on to the backing using the paper fasteners as the pivots. Make one of each type of lever.

4. Write on each strip where the effort and load are and draw arrows to show which way they move.

Make a list of any levers you can find in the garden, at home or in school. What jobs do the levers do?

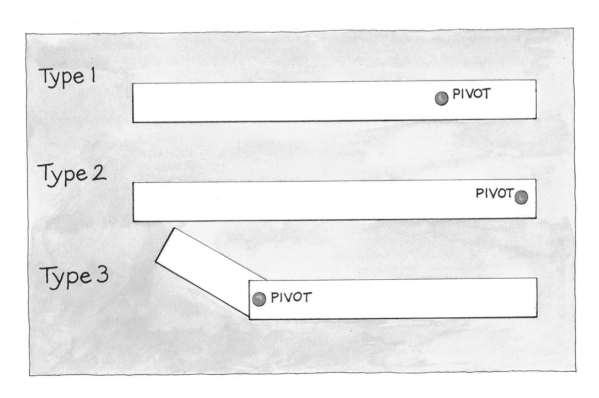

Notes for teachers and parents

What is spring? (Pages 6-7)
It is self-evident that most plants start their growth in the spring. They have been dormant during the winter in the form of seeds, bulbs or various root structures. Deciduous trees grow new leaves. Animal life also proliferates as spring approaches. Temperature obviously plays a large part in this process. Cold can and does kill off many young plants and animals. For wild animals and plants it is obviously better to come into the world when the temperature is warm and food is abundant. Although temperature is very important, it is known that day length also plays a part in triggering the mechanisms of growth and hibernation. Teachers need to be aware of this, although it is a difficult concept for young children to understand. They also need to take into account that in countries where there is little seasonal change it is the amount of food and water that affects growth.

Clouds and rain (Pages 8-9)
Clouds form in different patterns, often depending on the height at which they form. One of the highest, cirrus, is made up of ice crystals. Other factors which govern the types of clouds are the rates at which the air rises and just how much moisture it contains. When warm air rises it takes water vapour with it. When the air reaches a higher, and colder, level, the vapour condenses into water which falls as rain. The process is rarely as simple as this as various factors can influence the outcome. Temperature is one major ingredient. If the raindrops freeze the water will fall as hail, whereas if the water vapour itself freezes it falls as snow.

Recording the weather (Pages 10-11)
Seasonal changes are relatively constant, but weather can be unpredictable. Nevertheless, weather systems are governed by two major principles. One is that when air becomes warm, and hence lighter than cold air, it will rise. The other is that tightly packed air under high pressure will always flow outwards towards a low pressure area. It is very difficult to forecast the weather accurately and children need to understand that this is not what they are doing. They are, however, keeping a record of what is happening at the time. Apart from the technology and the record keeping involved, observing the weather in this way will help them to understand general climatic patterns. They may even discover that their local area has a microclimate all of its own.

Wind (Pages 12-13)
Wind is moving air. When air becomes warm it rises and cooler air moves in to take its place. This can occur on a very small scale producing a gentle local breeze, or it can happen on a global scale which provides a continual wind pattern. Small scale wind patterns can be found on coastlines when the sea breeze that blows during the day gives way to the land breeze in the evening. When measuring the speed and direction of the wind, children can relate it to both the temperature and to the cloud cover. They can decide if the wind affects the amount or type of cloud. If they notice a change in wind direction they may even be able to make short-term forecasts e.g. if a dry southerly breeze changes to a wet westerly wind.

Kites (Pages 14-15)
The simple act of flying a kite involves some sophisticated scientific principles. The same four forces are involved as in aeroplane flight (with which a useful comparison can be made). In the case of kite flying, *thrust* is the forward movement of the wind and *lift* is produced mainly by the deflection of this wind, hence the importance of the angle at which the kite is flying. *Drag* is produced by the pull of the string, — it can be measured by attaching a spring balance to the end of the string. *Gravity* will take over if there is no wind. Some children can understand these principles, especially when illustrated by the practical act of flying a kite. However, to keep the kite steady in the air all these forces have to be equal, and it is this balance of forces which children need to be aware of. Virtually the whole universe exists by keeping various similar forces in a state of balance.
Technical notes To measure the pull of wind on the kite, tie the end of the kite string to the hook of the spring balance. The position of the marker on the scale will vary with the strength of the wind. In strong winds it may be necessary to cut a V-shaped vent in the kite. This will help keep the kite at the correct flying angle. There is no need to cut the vent right out. Cut only two sides, so that in a gentle wind you can close the vent with masking tape.

Nests and houses (Pages 16-17)
Apart from the family pet, birds are often the most readily available animal for children to study. Even in the middle of the town it is possible to observe the habits and life-history of a selection of different types of bird. Their nests are particularly fascinating and children, while having regard to their safety, should be encouraged to observe not only how a nest is built, but the variety of materials used in their construction. It should be noted that not all birds build intricate nests. Many only arrange a few sticks on the ground and some may not even go this far. The experiment with the mud bricks will give the children the opportunity to devise a fair test. It is very important to eliminate all the variables in this kind of test. Dropping the weight down a tube will help keep the test accurate, as well as safeguarding the children from flying particles.

Frogs and tadpoles (Pages 18-19)

Frogs are amphibians, a biological group of animals that also includes toads, newts and salamanders. This group should *not* just be thought of as animals that can live on land and in the water. A penguin could be included under that definition. It does not fly, but it is an excellent swimmer and this is how it catches its food. However, it nests on land, lays a hard-shelled egg and is obviously a bird. Amphibians have two major characteristics: (i) the first part of their life cycle is always spent in the water, (ii) although some of them may have lungs, when out of water they mainly breathe through their skins, for which purpose the skin has to be kept moist. Children need to know something of the frog's physiology so that they can better look after the animal. They should understand that while some amphibians, such as newts, will spend most of their life in water, others such as salamanders and even toads, will only return to the water to breed. Some frogs live like this as well so it is very important not to keep adult frogs permanently in water; they must have stones or sticks to help them climb out of the water.

Spring flowers (Pages 20-21)

Pollen is present in the air in large quantities as early as February. Hazel trees, for example, produce large amounts of pollen early in the year which is carried by the wind. Later in the year, most wind-borne pollen comes from grass. The flowers of wind pollinated plants can do without petals. The majority of coloured flowers, however, are pollinated by insects which are attracted by their brightly coloured petals. It is pollen from these flowers that is easy to collect and observe. Pollen and ovary are not always found in the same flower. Some species have two types of flower on the same plant. The Hazel tree has pollen on the catkin which is blown to a small red flower, often on the same branch. It is this flower that has the ovary that produces the seed in the form of a nut. Other species, such as the Holly, have two different flowers on entirely separate plants. The sticky-backed plastic will collect pollen and also any other particles that are in the air. Children can design ways to measure this pollution. One method is to shine a light through the plastic. The amount of light that passes through can be measured by a meter. The plastic will be very dirty if there is much pollution, and the light passing through will be reduced.

Growing seeds (Pages 22-23)

Children should always experience the excitement of growing their own plants. In the first experiment they can also discover the best conditions for plant growth. Make sure that when the seeds are first sown, they are all given a thorough watering. Subsequent watering must be done at regular intervals, each tray receiving the same amount. Further experiments can be carried out using different concentrations of plant food to see which one produces the best growth. All green plants fall into two main groups, based on their number of seed leaves (cotyledons). Monocotyledons, such as grass and maize, have one, while most other flowering plants, such as the broad bean, are dicotyledonous and have two. These seed leaves are the first to develop and play an important part in providing food for the growing seed. In the second experiment, children can also observe how the growing roots develop. Maize has an extensive root system, while the broad bean has a central tap root system. Children should note the fine hairs at the tips of the roots. It is through these that moisture and soluble minerals are taken into the plant. Both seeds are readily available from garden centres.

The greenhouse (Pages 24-25)

A fully heated greenhouse will allow a gardener to grow a wide range of plants, many of them tropical, throughout the year. Children can make a simple greenhouse themselves which, when placed outside can protect plants from early frosts, or, when inside a warm classroom, will act as a heated greenhouse or propagator. The plastic should reach down to just below the top rim of the tray. This will make for easy access to the plants and allow good circulation of air. Make sure that water can drain away through the sand or gravel. Without adequate ventilation and drainage the inside of the greenhouse will become very wet. Fungi and algae will grow and in time will kill the plants. Moisture will accumulate not only from plant water, but also from the moisture given out as part of photosynthesis, from the leaves themselves. This 'invisible' moisture will condense on the inside of the plastic and needs to be able to drain away. A more permanent structure can be made using square section wood supported at the corners with small triangles of cardboard. Make the structure as rigid as possible using cross pieces to support the plastic. It can then be taken outside and the cover will not blow away nor will it collapse if it rains.

The Greenhouse Effect There are different 'kinds' of heat. Infra-red heat can pass through glass. This is taken in by the soil and the plants. The plants give out their own energy, but at a longer wavelength which cannot pass freely through the glass. In this way the temperature in a greenhouse can be as much as 15° C higher than that outside. We want the greenhouse to be warm and it is worth remembering that the Earth's Greenhouse Effect is necessary to keep us warm, too. Without it, the surface of the Earth would be many degrees cooler. However, like an unventilated greenhouse in hot weather, the Earth could itself overheat. Carbon-dioxide and water vapour act like glass. They absorb heat and send it back down to Earth. With the increase of carbon-dioxide in the atmosphere, less heat escapes.

Levers (Pages 26-27)

Because a first type lever is the most efficient, it is the one to use in any situation if possible. Types two and three are adaptations to specific designs, and type three is even mechanically inefficient. Ask the children to try to design an arm using one of the other types of lever.

Further reading

Bates, Jeffrey, *Hands on Science: Seeds to Plants* (Franklin Watts, 1990)

Taylor–Cork, Barbara, *Be an Expert Weather* Forecaster (Gloucester Press, 1992)

Tomson, Ruth, *Spring* (Franklin Watts, 1989)

Yorke, Jane, *My First Look At: Seasons* (Dorling Kindersley, 1990)

Association for Science Education, *Be Safe*, 2nd edition (1990)

Glossary

Absorb To take in or soak up a liquid or a gas. A sponge absorbs water, which is a liquid.

Aerobatic The special movements that an aeroplane makes when it is performing stunts at a flying display. You can make a kite perform some of these movements.

Experiment A test made to discover something that is not known.

Germinate This is when seeds first begin to grow into plants.

Gills Parts of the body of animals that live in water. These parts have a special skin that takes in oxygen from the water so that the animal can breathe.

Gauge A tool for measuring the size or amount of something.

Life cycle The normal way that an animal or plant develops.

Lungs Parts of the body with which most land animals breathe.

North and South Poles The most northerly and southerly places on the Earth. They form either end of the axis on which the Earth spins.

Temperature How hot or cold something is.

SCIENCE FUN THROUGH THE SEASONS

Summer

Science Projects

SCIENCE FUN THROUGH THE SEASONS

Summer

Science Projects

Notes on the National Curriculum

The specific references in this section are made to programmes of study. However, all the work in this book is compatible with the attainment targets for science, levels 1–5. Teachers will therefore be able to make their own judgements concerning individual pupils based on their ability to carry out these projects.

Experimental and investigative science
All the practical work in this book, the experimenting, testing and recording meet many of the requirements of this programme of study, at both key stages 1 and 2.

The details of other programmes of study are listed under individual sections.

What is summer?
Life processes and living things (key stages 1 and 2)
Materials and their properties (key stage 2)
Physical processes (key stage 2)
There are cross-curricular links with geography.

Hot air rises
Materials and their properties (key stages 1 and 2)
Physical processes (key stage 2)
There are cross-curricular links with technology and mathematics.

Evaporation and The salty sea
Materials and their properties (key stages 1 and 2)
Physical processes (key stages 1 and 2)
There are cross-curricular links with geography.

Floating in the sea and Sailing boats
Materials and their properties (key stages 1 and 2)
Physical processes (key stages 1 and 2)
There are strong cross-curricular links with technology.

Plants in summer and Plants need water
Life processes and living things (key stages 1 and 2)
Materials and their properties (key stage 2)
There are cross-curricular links with geography.

Watering the fields and The shadoof
Life processes and living things (key stages 1 and 2)
Physical processes (key stages 1 and 2)
There are cross-curricular links with technology, history, geography and RE.

Contents

*****   Words in bold in the text are explained in the glossary.

What is summer?

There are four seasons — spring, summer, autumn and winter. Summer is the hottest season of the year.

Here are two signs that summer has come:
■ There are flowers blooming in parks and gardens.
■ It stays light until quite late in the evening.
Can you think of any more?

Right: For both players and spectators light, white clothes are best in summer.
Below: A garden in full summer bloom.

In the summer people often wear white or light coloured clothes. This project will help you understand why.

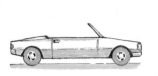

PROJECT: Colour and temperature

You will need

- Shallow lids from two boxes, for example, shoe boxes
- About 1kg of black powder paint
- About 1kg of plaster of Paris powder
- 2 soil thermometers

What to do

1. Fill one box lid with a 3cm thick layer of powder paint and the other with a 3cm layer of plaster of Paris powder.

2. Place the two box lids on the ground outside, or on a sunny windowsill.

3. Use the soil thermometers to measure the temperature of the powders every hour for one or two days.

Which box gets warmest?

Draw a chart like this one to show the differences in temperature.

Time	Temperature in °C	
	Black box	White box
9. 00am		
10. 00am		
11. 00am		

Go out into the school car park on a hot day. Feel the cars. Which ones are warmer to the touch, the dark coloured ones or the light coloured ones?

Why do you think some colours get hotter than others?

Hot air rises

Hot air rises. Even small amounts of air warmed by a radiator will float upwards. Large amounts of moving warm air are called **thermals.**

These balloons float because they are filled with hot air.

Project: Make a hot air balloon

You will need
- Five sheets of tissue paper each about 75cm x 50cm
- A pencil
- Scissors
- Glue
- A hair dryer

What to do

1. Fold a sheet of paper in half. Then in half again and then in half again.

2. Unfold the sheet to show a pattern. Use the pattern to cut out the shape shown in the diagram opposite.

3. Repeat these steps for three of the other sheets. These are the sides of your balloon.

4. Cut a 50cm square from the fifth piece of tissue paper. This will be the top of your balloon.

5. Glue the four sides to the edges of this square.

6. Hold the sides of the balloon together and stick them with glue.

7. Cut a 25cm square of tissue paper. Cut a hole in the middle. Stick this square to the bottom of the balloon.

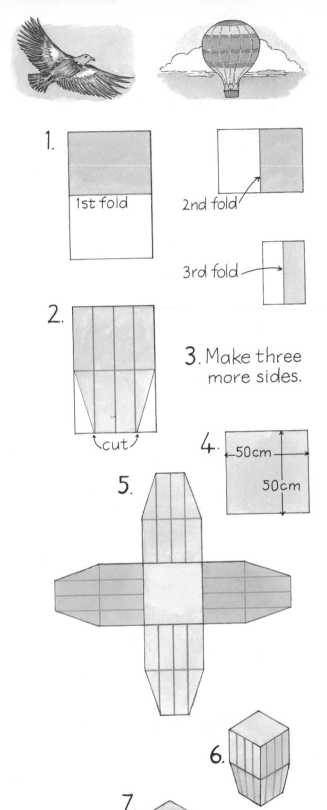

1.

1st fold

2nd fold

3rd fold

2.

3. Make three more sides.

cut

4. 50cm 50cm

5.

6.

7.

8. Place the nozzle of the hair dryer in the hole at the base of the balloon and blow hot air into it. Hold it there for several minutes until you feel the tug of the balloon.

9. When the sides of the balloon are quite hot, let it go. How high does it fly?

Evaporation

After it has rained, the trees, grass and playgound are very wet. When the sun shines everything dries out again. This experiment will help you find out how quickly the sun dries things.

PROJECT: Drying a puddle

You will need
- A playground puddle
- A piece of chalk
- A sunny day!

What to do

1. Draw around the edge of the puddle with the chalk. Mark the time next to the chalk outline.

2. Come back every hour, marking the new outline and time, until the puddle has disappeared.

How long did the puddle take to dry? Where do you think the water in the puddle has gone?

When it is very hot our bodies sweat. As the sweat **evaporates**, it cools us down. Very large animals need more than sweat to keep themselves cool. Elephants have ears that act like car **radiators**. They spread out their ears so that the wind can cool the blood that runs through them.

The wind can also help to dry things as this project will show.

PROJECT: Drying in the wind

You will need
- Some pieces of cotton cloth, all 30cm x 30cm
- Clothes pegs

What to do

1. Soak all the pieces of cloth in water. Do not squeeze the water out.

2. Peg them on to fences or on trees in different parts of the playground or garden. Make sure you peg them: in the shade; in the sun; in the shade with the wind; in the sun with the wind. You could also hang some indoors.

Which one takes longest to dry? Which one dries the quickest?

The salty sea

Many people like to take holidays by the sea in summer. We know that there is salt in sea water because we can taste it when we swim. We can't see the salt because the little pieces in the water are too small.

PROJECT: Getting salt from sea water

You will need
- Salt
- A container of water
- Several plastic saucers
- A magnifying glass
- A clear plastic bag

What to do

1. Stir salt into the container of water until all of it has disappeared.

2. Pour the salt water carefully into each of the saucers and stand the saucers outside in the sun or on a sunny windowsill.

3. When the saucers are dry, look at what is left in them under a magnifying glass.

What you can see are **crystals** of salt. What shape are the crystals? Can you explain what has happened?

Do this experiment again using different amounts of salt. Try using other mixtures, like sugar or bath crystals. Do they work in the same way as salt?

Now repeat the experiment but this time place a clear plastic bag over the saucer. You can tuck the plastic bag under the saucer to stop it blowing away.

What do you notice appearing on the inside of the plastic bag as the water in the saucer dries up?

You are seeing the water cycle in action. The picture below shows you how it works in real life.

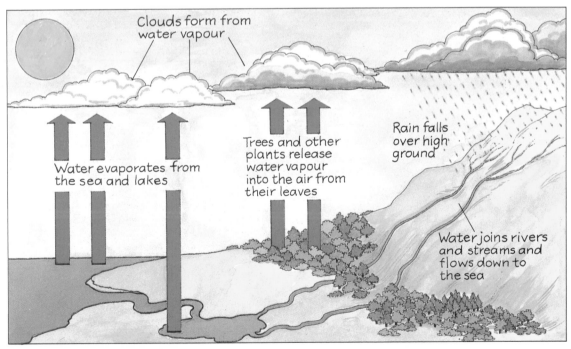

Clouds form from water vapour

Water evaporates from the sea and lakes

Trees and other plants release water vapour into the air from their leaves

Rain falls over high ground

Water joins rivers and streams and flows down to the sea

Floating in the sea

Swimming in the sea is easier than swimming in fresh water. Ships float at different levels in salt and fresh water, too. This experiment shows how salt in the water helps keep us and ships afloat.

It's easy to float in the Dead Sea because it is so salty.

PROJECT: Floating in the sea

You will need
- A drinking straw
- Plasticine
- 2 plastic aquarium tanks, one of fresh and one of salt water

What to do

1. Fix a small ball of Plasticine to the end of one of the drinking straws.

2. Put the straw in the tank of fresh water so that it floats upright.

3. Put a mark on the straw at the water level.

4. Now do the same for the tank of salt water.

How far apart are the marks on the straw? How much of the straw is under in fresh and in salt water?

Fill an aquarium with even saltier water and repeat the experiment. Does the extra salt make any difference?

Sailing boats

This is a sailing regatta in the Baltic Sea. How do the yachts manage to stay upright?

Summer is a good time for sailing model boats and real yachts. Racing yachts have long, thin **hulls** and tall sails.

How do they stay upright in the water when the wind is blowing and the sea is rough?

PROJECT: Testing hulls

You will need
- Two sheets of balsa wood, one 20cm long, 0.5cm thick and 10cm wide, and one 20cm long, 0.5 cm thick and 5cm wide
- Three pieces of wooden dowel, two 20cm long and one 35cm long
- Plasticine and sticky tape
- A modelling knife and metal ruler
- Some sheets of paper
- Scissors and a pencil

What to do

1. Cut a point at one end of each piece of balsa wood. These are your **bows**.

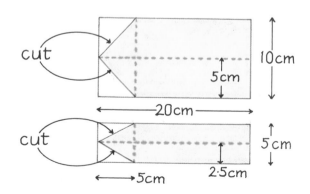

2. Use the pencil to make a hole in the middle of both pieces of wood 8cm from the bow. Push a 20cm dowel through each hole for masts.

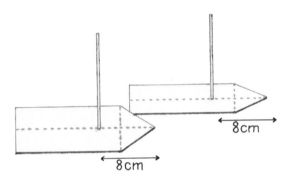

8cm

8cm

3. Make a paper sail for each boat and float them in water. Which one stays upright?

4. Replace the mast on the narrow boat with the longer dowel, leaving about 15cm under the boat.

5. Fix a small ball of Plasticine to the bottom of the dowel. Does the boat stay upright now?

Look at pictures of real yachts. What shape are the parts that are under the water?

WARNING: ASK AN ADULT TO HELP YOU CUT THE BALSA WOOD.

49

Catamarans

Catamarans have two hulls and trimarans have three.

Some sailing boats have more than one hull. Those that have two hulls are called catamarans. Those that have three are called trimarans.

PROJECT: Make a catamaran

You will need
- Two square-shaped plastic bottles
- A sheet of balsa wood 10cm wide, 0.5cm thick and 35cm long
- Four 35cm lengths of 1cm x 1cm balsa wood
- One piece of dowel about 40cm long
- Rubber bands
- A sheet of paper
- Scissors and sticky tape
- A pencil

What to do

1. Using the rubber bands, fix the sheet of balsa wood across the bottles. The bottles should be about 15 cm apart.

2. Fix the long square pieces of wood across each end of the bottles, on both the top and bottom, with more rubber bands.

3. Use the pencil to make a hole in the middle of the balsa wood. Fix the dowel mast into the hole.

4. Cut a sail from the sheet of paper. Stick it to the mast.

WARNING: ASK AN ADULT TO HELP YOU CUT THE BALSA WOOD.

Does your model float upright in the water?

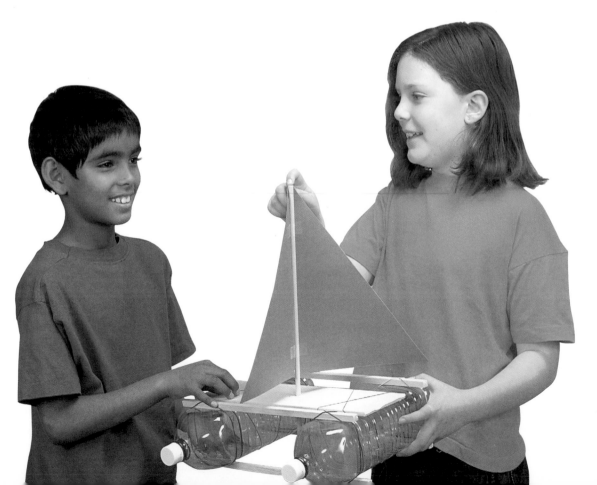

Plants in summer

All plants need water to stay alive. Sometimes, during a dry summer, we have to water our gardens with a watering can or hosepipe. Plants collect the water in the ground through their roots. Then it travels up through their stems.

Project: Plants in water

You will need
- Some white summer flowers like carnations or large daisies
- A jar full of water coloured with ink or food colouring

What to do

Place the flowers in the jar of coloured water and leave them there for a day. What happens to the colour of the flowers?

Try the experiment with different food colourings. Which ones work best?

Plants do not keep all the water they take in. Some of the water escapes through little holes in their leaves, called stomata. Stomata can close up during the day to help save water.

Project: Collecting water from plants

You will need
- A plant in a pot
- A plastic bag
- Sticky tape
- A watch

What to do

1. Put the plastic bag over the pot plant.

2. Fix the bag tightly around the stem of the plant with the sticky tape. Be careful not to damage the plant.

3. Measure the time it takes for water to collect on the inside of the bag.

4. Now fix a bag over just one leaf of another plant of the same type.

How much water comes from one leaf?

Try the experiment with a different plant. Does water appear in the bag at the same time?

Imagine how much water comes from a large tree or a forest of trees. Where does all the water go (see page 45)?

Plants need water

Summers can be very dry. Many plants have special leaves to help them keep the water inside. You can find out which leaves keep water the longest.

Project: Drying leaves

You will need
- Lots of different leaves
- Cotton thread
- Two short garden canes

What to do

1. Tie the thread between the canes. Then push the canes into the ground in a warm place where there is a breeze.

2. Tie the leaves on to the thread.

3. Look at the leaves every hour. Keep a record like this of how they change.

Changes in the leaf after every hour.	Type and shape of leaf	
	Holly	Oak
1 hour colour shape feel		
2 hours colour shape feel		

We have seen how plants both take in and let out water. You can make a small self-contained world where you can watch them doing this.

Project: Make a bottle garden

You will need
- A large plastic sweet jar with a wide neck
- A pack of clean potting soil from a garden centre
- Charcoal and small pebbles
- Some small plants like ivy, ferns and mosses
- About 250ml of water

What to do

1. Spread the pebbles on the bottom of the jar. Then put a layer of charcoal on top of the pebbles.

2. Sprinkle about 10cm of soil on to the charcoal.

3. Carefully take your plants out of their pots and plant them in the soil.

4. Water the soil but don't make it too wet.

5. Replace the lid and put your bottle garden in a warm, bright place, but not in direct sunlight.

Your plants should need no further attention.

55

Watering the fields

All crops need water or they will die. In countries where the summers are very dry water has to be brought up from wells deep underground.

The water can be pumped up by hand, by animal power, by a windmill or by a machine.

You can make a cardboard model of a hand pump.

At this traditional 'Persian well' in India, the oxen provide the power to lift the water.

PROJECT: A model hand pump

You will need
- Thin card
- Paper fasteners
- Crayons or felt-tip pens
- Scissors
- A pencil
- A ruler

What to do

1. Cut a piece of card for the backing 20cm x 18cm.

2. Cut a handle 20cm long and 3cm wide. Cut a piston 14cm long, 2cm wide along most of its length and 3cm wide' at the end. Colour them both.

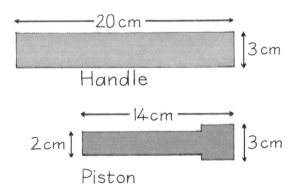

Handle

Piston

3. Make a hole in the handle, 1cm from the end and another 6cm from the end.

4. Make a hole in the backing card about 4cm in from the left hand side and 3cm from the top.

5. Fix the handle on to the backing card with a paper fastener.

6. Make a hole in the top of the piston. Then lay it in position over the handle. Mark and cut out two slits about two-thirds of the way down the backing card.

7. Thread the piston up through the slits. Fix it to the handle with a paper fastener.

8. Draw the well shaft on the backing paper. Colour the water blue.

What happens to the piston when you move the handle up and down?

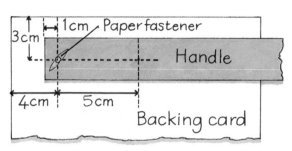

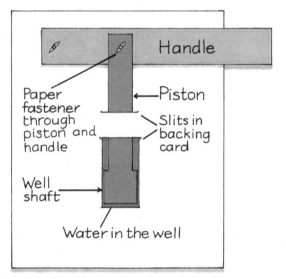

What would happen to the water in a real well if a piston was pushed down?

A shadoof

In some countries, like Egypt and India, a simple lever is used to bring water up from wells underground. The water is then used to **irrigate** the fields. The lever is called a shadoof and has been in use for thousands of years.

You can make your own model shadoof.

This Egyptian man is using a shadoof to raise water from a well to water his crops. The weight of water is balanced by the rocks at the other end of the lever.

PROJECT: Make a shadoof

You will need
- 3 pieces of 1cm x 1cm balsa wood, two 8cm long and one 18cm long
- A piece of thick card or balsa wood 10cm x 10cm
- Plasticine
- Scissors
- About 20cm of cotton thread
- A long pin or needle
- Glue
- A small piece of kitchen foil

What to do

1. Push the pin through the top of one of the short pieces of wood 2cm from the end.

2. Now push the pin through the long piece of wood about 5cm from the end. This piece will form the lever.

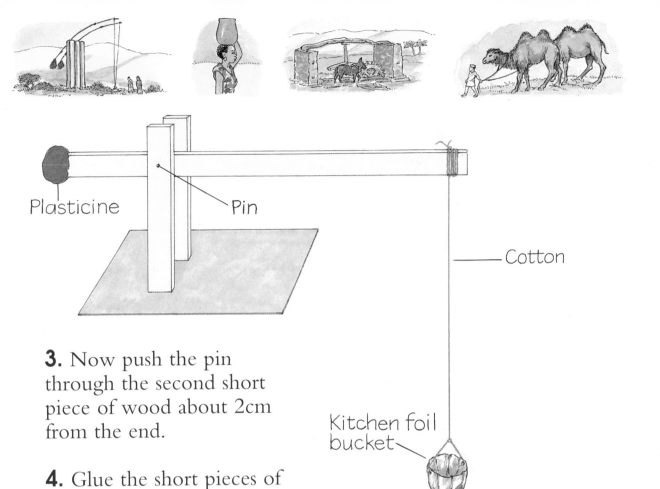

Plasticine

Pin

Cotton

Kitchen foil bucket

3. Now push the pin through the second short piece of wood about 2cm from the end.

4. Glue the short pieces of wood on to the card.

5. Glue or tie the cotton to the long end of the lever.

6. Make a little bucket from the piece of kitchen foil and tie or glue this to the other end of the cotton thread.

7. Balance the lever at its short end with Plasticine.

When the lever is balanced a heavy bucket of water can be lifted easily.

59

Notes for teachers and parents

Colour and temperature (Pages 38-39)

Objects receive heat from the sun through the process of radiation. It is the infrared radiation from the sun that warms us. This kind of radiation behaves in the same way as light, and can even be reflected and focused by a mirror. Shiny surfaces are good reflectors, while dull surfaces absorb the heat. Conversely, dull surfaces are better emitters of heat than shiny surfaces. Hence a hot liquid will retain its heat better in a shiny container than in a dark one. This should be understood when measuring the temperature of the two 'soils'. The temperature just above the surface may be similar — the light coloured one because of the reflection of heat, and the dark coloured one because of the heat emitted from it. However, the temperature inside the 'soils' should show a difference.

Hot air rises (Pages 40-41)

Children may understand that hot air rises, but they may not know why. As with other substances, heated air molecules vibrate more vigorously, and draw apart from one another. In this way, warm air becomes lighter and will rise up and float above cold, denser air. The hot air in the balloon will actually have less molecules compared with the equivalent volume of air outside. So it will float upwards in just the same way as a boat floats on water.

Making a hot air balloon can give rise to many cross-curricular activities. Children can be given the opportunity to study technology and design, the history of flight, weather and even mathematics. When making the balloon, children can begin to understand the concept of volume. They can make connections between volume and surface area, and make calculations such as what happens to the volume if the dimensions of the balloon are doubled or halved.

Evaporation (Pages 42-43)

Evaporation is the changing of a liquid into a vapour. There is almost instant evaporation when a liquid boils, but of course it does not have to reach this temperature before evaporation takes place. When a substance is heated the molecules inside it vibrate more and more quickly. Some molecules near the surface of the liquid may have enough energy to escape. This can happen at any temperature, although obviously the hotter it is the quicker the rate of evaporation.

Children should understand that just because the water in the puddle reduces, it has not, as it may seem to them, disappeared into thin air. It has just changed its state. This is because it is the hotter molecules that escape, leaving behind the cooler ones. On a hot day this can keep us cool, but in cold, windy conditions it can be dangerous, and the heat loss can be very considerable. The action of the wind is always an important factor in the process of evaporation. Elsewhere in this book (**Plants need water**), there are examples of how plants protect their leaves from the wind. They try to create little pockets of humid air near the stomata. In the case of most animals, their problem is to stop themselves overheating in hot weather. The ears of an elephant act like a car radiator. As the ears spread out, the blood in the capillaries cools. Unlike the leaves of plants, any movement or air in these circumstances is welcome.

Salt from sea water (Pages 44-45)

This is another evaporation experiment. However the emphasis changes to discovering what solids remain when all the water is gone. It would be helpful if the children had some previous experience of dissolving solids in water. They will then already know that some solids will normally fully dissolve in water, so that none of the particles can be seen, and the original solid cannot easily be retrieved.

Other substances, however, do not dissolve fully. Instead, they remain as small particles suspended in the water. These particles can easily be retrieved by filtration. Salt is a chemical that does dissolve in water. Filtration will have no effect on the solution. Once the water has evaporated away, however, the salt will remain, ideally as small, cube-shaped crystals.

The final experiment in this section should help reinforce the idea that the water is still around, although as a vapour and not a liquid. Like the water from the transpiration experiments later in the book, it is not until it cools down that it will condense back into water.

Floating in water (Pages 46-47)

Children may often experiment with a variety of objects to find out if they will float or sink, but it is unlikely that they will do more than list two sets. It is much more difficult to understand how things float, and it is unreasonable to expect young children to manage this concept. When an object is placed on water, gravity would normally pull it down. However, there is an opposing push or upthrust which may keep the object afloat. Children can feel this upthrust by trying to push a piece of wood or plastic underwater. This is not, however, the whole story. A brick weighing 2.5 kg placed in a tank of water will seem to lose at least a kilogram of its weight, but it still will not sink. Only if the brick could be spread thinly over the water, so that the upthrust was greater per given area of brick, would it float.

Children do not have to understand the theory, but they can experiment with this idea. A lump of Plasticine dropped into a tank of water will sink. However, if it is formed into a saucer-shaped boat, it will float. Because salt water is more dense that fresh water, the upthrust will be greater. The drinking straws are a form of crude hydrometer. They will float higher in salt water and even higher in very salty water.

Stability in water (Pages 48-51)

These two sections are about stability in water, particularly sailing yachts, which often have a very slim hull, and yet have a tall mast and a large area of sail. Most sailing boats manage with ballast to stop them capsizing. Racing yachts, however, require a deep keel, often tipped with lead. When the wind pushes on one side of the sails, there is a push from the water on the opposite side of the keel, so keeping the boat upright.

The experiments in this project will help children understand the technology.

Catamarans are often more stable than craft with a single hull. Even with a basic model such as this, stability should not be a problem. Children can choose between two basic sail patterns — the square rig and the fore-and-aft rig. They should understand that all the various pushes and pulls of the wind on the sails, and the water on the boat, are all examples of forces.

NOTE: A modelling knife should always be used in conjunction with a metal ruler. Both as a safeguard and a guide, the blade should be held against the edge of the ruler.

Plants in summer (Pages 52-55)

These two sections look at how plants take in and lose water and how they avoid losing water during times of drought. Plants can lose as much as 90 per cent of their total water through transpiration. This is the loss of water, mainly through the stomata, that is necessary in order that other water can be drawn up the stem. The stomata have to stay open for at least part of the day, to allow the passage of oxygen and carbon dioxide during respiration and photosynthesis.

In times of water shortage, plants need to cut down on loss through transpiration. The xerophytes (eg cacti), are a very specialized group of plants, adapted to survive under extreme conditions. They have special water storage cells, their leaves are reduced to sharp spines and their stomata rarely open during the day. Other plants may not be so specialized, but they nonetheless often need to cope with temporary water shortages.

One of the most common adaptations is a leathery and often waxy cuticle. The stomata is often at the base of a small pit, so protecting it from moving air. The holly is one such plant. Other ways in which plants cut down water loss is by having hair-like structures in the leaves, or to have folded or rolled up leaves. The oleander is a good example of a plant with a hairy leaf, while many grasses have rolled up leaves.

The terrarium should be a balanced plant community. It can include some small invertebrates, so as to make it into a biotope — a small area in which plants and animals with similar habitats can live together as a balanced ecological community.

Raising water (Pages 56-59)

In the first of these two sections a model shows how a piston works in conjunction with a lever handle. In a real pump there are two valves — one is the piston and one in the base of the barrel. When the piston moves down the lower valve closes, but the piston valve opens. When this happens, water enters the top of the pump and out of the spout. Because water is raised by atmospheric pressure, a pump of this kind cannot raise water by more than 10 metres. If children are aware of the three different kinds of levers they should be able to decide which type of lever is used for the handle of this model and whether other types of lever could be used instead.

Shadoofs can be found in use today along the banks of rivers in the Middle East, India and Egypt. They are used for raising water over a short distance and are based on the balanced lever principle. The shadoof is a type one lever, where the fulcrum is anywhere between the effort and the load. It is balanced so that it needs only a light touch to raise the load of water. Levers in general do not have to be balanced in this way, it just depends on what they are designed to do.

Further reading

Fitzgerald, Janet, *Science Through the Seasons: Summer in the Wood* (Evans, 1992)

Harlow, Rosie and Morgan, Gareth, *Fun With Science: The Seasons* (Kingfisher, 1991)

Pluckrose, Henry, *Changing Seasons* (Franklin Watts, 1993)

Woolfitt, Gabrielle, *Science Through the Seasons: Summer* (Wayland, 1995)

Association for Science Education, *Be Safe,* 2nd edition (1990)

Glossary

Bows The front part of a boat, usually pointed in shape.

Crystal A regular shaped solid. Crystals can be coloured or clear. Diamonds are a kind of crystal.

Evaporate To turn from a liquid or solid into a vapour.

Hull The main body of a boat to which the other parts, such as the mast and rudder, are fixed.

Irrigate To supply land and crops with water.

Radiator Something which gives out heat. A car radiator gets rid of the heat from the water that cools the engine.

Thermal Anything to do with heat. A mass of warm air rising above the ground.

SCIENCE FUN THROUGH THE SEASONS

Autumn

Science Projects

SCIENCE FUN THROUGH THE SEASONS

Autumn

Science Projects

Notes on the National Curriculum

The specific references in this section are made to programmes of study. However, all the work in this book is compatible with the attainment targets for science, levels 1-5. Teachers will therefore be able to make their own judgements concerning individual pupils based on their ability to carry out these projects.

Experimental and investigative science
All the practical work in this book, the experimenting, testing and recording, meet many of the requirements of this programme of study, at both key stages 1 and 2.

The details of other programmes of study are listed under individual sections.

What is autumn?
Life processes and living things (key stages 1 and 2)
There are cross-curricular links with geography.

Autumn fruits
Life processes and living things (key stages 1 and 2)
There are cross-curricular links with technology.

Fruit stains
Materials and their properties (general background))

Are fruits acid?
Materials and their properties (general background)

How seeds spread
Life processes and living things (key stages 1 and 2)
Materials and their properties (general background)
There are cross-curricular links with technology.

Plants without seeds
Life processes and living things (key stages 1 and 2)

Birds and flight *and* **Looking at feathers**
Life processes and living things (key stages 1 and 2)
There are cross-curricular links with technology.

Gliders
Materials and their properties (key stages 1 and 2)
Physical processes (key stages 1 and 2)
There are cross-curricular links with technology.

The night sky
There are cross-curricular links with technology and geography.

Animals in autumn
Life processes and living things (key stages 1 and 2)

Contents

* Words in bold in the text are explained in the glossary.

What is autumn?

There are four seasons — spring, summer, autumn and winter. In autumn, the air begins to get cooler. Animals and plants start to get ready for winter.

Here are two signs that autumn has come:
- The leaves on some trees begin to turn red, orange or brown.
- It begins to get dark earlier in the evenings.

Can you think of any more?

Autumn is also called the 'fall'. Why do you think this name is used?

Autumn is not the same everywhere. In some countries it can be a very short season. You can find out which countries have long autumns and which ones have short autumns.

Autumn is the time of year when the leaves on some trees start to turn red, orange or brown.

Project: Autumn around the world

You will need
- A world map or globe
- A notebook and pencil

What to do

1. Find the **lines of latitude** called the tropics of Cancer and Capricorn on your map or globe.

The countries between these two lines have warm weather almost all the year round. This region is called the tropics.

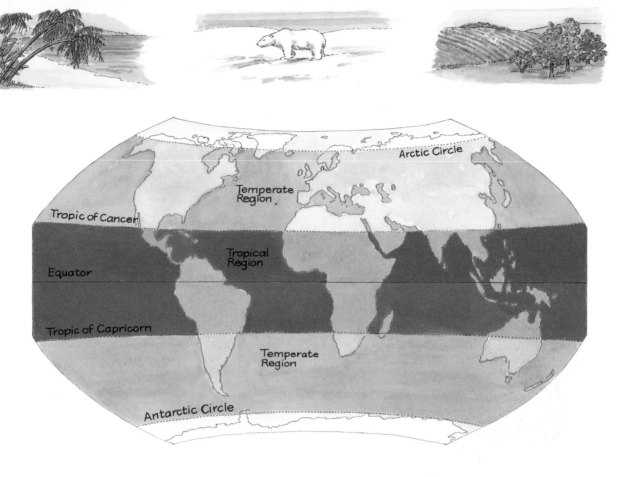

Arctic Circle

Temperate Region

Tropic of Cancer

Tropical Region

Equator

Tropic of Capricorn

Temperate Region

Antarctic Circle

2. Now look for the lines of latitude called the **Arctic** and **Antarctic** circles.

The countries to the north of the Arctic Circle and south of the Antarctic Circle have little or no autumn. They have short summers and long winters.

3. Make a list of the countries between the Arctic Circle and the Tropic of Cancer and those between the Tropic of Capricorn and the Antarctic Circle.

These are the temperate countries, where there will be a long autumn.

Autumn fruits

Many different kinds of fruit are picked in the autumn. The fruit is the part of a plant that carries the seeds.

Harvesting apples in autumn.

There are many different types of fruits. Here are three types that you might find:

Berries are soft fruits that often have many little seeds covered by a thin skin. Tomatoes and gooseberries are berries.

Pods are long, narrow fruits, with a row of seeds inside. Peas and runner beans grow in pods.

Drupes are soft fruits with a hard stone inside. The stone has the seed inside it. There is only one seed in each stone. Cherries and plums are drupes.

Project: Collecting fruits

1. Make a collection of as many different fruits as you can find. Look in hedgerows and your garden as well as the supermarket.

2. Divide your collection into berries, pods and drupes.

3. Ask an adult to help you cut the fruits open. Can you find the seeds? How many seeds are there? Are they big or small, hard or soft?

4. Make drawings of the cut halves of fruits.

Project: Making fruit prints

You will need
- Different kinds of hard fruits, like apples and pears
- Paper
- A knife
- Paint and a paintbrush
- Saucers to mix paint in

What to do

1. Ask an adult to cut the fruits in half down the middle.

2. Cover the cut half with paint and press it down on to the paper. Do this all over your paper to make a pattern. Try using different coloured paints.

Fruit stains

If you have been out picking blackberries, you will find your fingers are coloured blue. This is the juice of the berry. If it stains your clothes it is very difficult to remove.

Blackberries are a sure sign of autumn and are a delicious feast for people, animals and birds.

Project: Removing fruit stains

You will need
- Some pieces of old, white cotton sheet, all about 20cm x 20cm
- Plastic pots or cups
- Warm water
- Juice squeezed from blackberries, blackcurrants or some other soft fruit
- Some different kinds of washing powder
- A teaspoon

What to do

1. Put one drop of fruit juice in the middle of each piece of cloth.

2. Pour equal amounts of warm water into each cup.

3. Stir a small teaspoonful of the different powders into each of the cups but leave one cup with no washing powder in it at all. Label the cups carefully.

4. Put a cotton square into each cup. Stir for ten minutes.

5. Take out the pieces of cloth and dry them.

Have any of the stains faded?

Have any of them disappeared altogether? What happened to the cloth in the cup with no washing powder?

Arrange the cloths in order from most to least faded.

Are fruits acid?

Many fruits can taste sour. This may be because they are not ripe. But some fruits, such as lemons, limes and even some oranges are always sour. The sourness is caused by chemicals in the fruit called acids.

Project: Testing for acids

You will need
- Some clear plastic cups
- Some fruit. Try a lemon, an orange and blackberries
- Litmus paper

What to do

1. Squeeze a little fruit juice into each of the containers, one juice for each cup.

2. Dip a piece of blue **litmus** paper into each of the cups.

If the paper turns red, the juice is an acid. If the paper stays the same colour, it is not.

Did all the juices turn the litmus paper red?

Project: Make your own acid indicator

You will need
- Red cabbage leaves or dahlia petals
- A bowl
- A short piece of smooth stick
- A little water
- A plastic cup

What to do

1. Squash the red cabbage leaves or dahlia petals with a little water, using the piece of smooth stick.

2. Collect the liquid in the plastic cup. This is your acid **indicator**.

What colour is the liquid?

3. Pour a little of the liquid into each of your fruit juice samples.

Do the samples change colour?

Compare the colours that your home-made indicator gives compared to the litmus paper.

Can you tell if the fruit juices are acid using your home-made indicator?

Can you tell how strong the acid is?

How seeds spread

When seeds are ripe they must be planted. However, if the seeds just fell all together around the parent plant they would not be able to grow well. They will grow better if they are spread around, or dispersed. This is done in many ways.

Look at your fruit collection. How do you think the seeds inside them are dispersed?

Some trees, such as the ash, plane, sycamore and maple have seeds with wings. These fly like helicopters and land many metres from the tree.

You can experiment with flying seeds.

Project: Flying seeds

You will need
- Some different sorts of seeds with wings
- A chair
- A long tape measure

What to do

1. Take your seeds out into the playground or garden. Stand on the chair and throw them into the air, one at a time. How do they fly?

2. Use your tape measure to measure how far each seed flies. You can record your results on a bar graph like the one below.

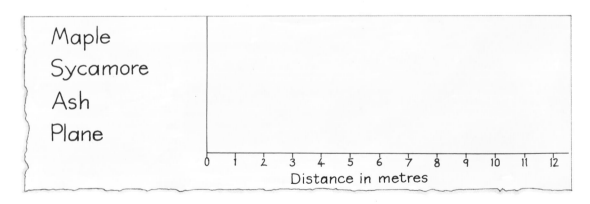

Maple
Sycamore
Ash
Plane

0 1 2 3 4 5 6 7 8 9 10 11 12
Distance in metres

Project: Make your own sycamore seed

You will need
- Some stiff card about 15cm x 5cm
- Plasticine
- A straw
- Glue
- A chair

3. Glue the Plasticine to the end of the wing to form the seed. Twist the wing into the shape of a propeller.

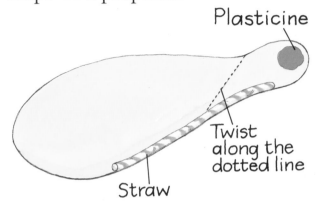

Plasticine

Twist along the dotted line

Straw

What to do

1. Cut the card into the shape of a sycamore wing.

2. Bend the straw into the shape of one edge of the wing and glue it to that edge.

4. Stand on a chair and drop the seed.

You can make several models of different sizes. Which one flies the best?

Plants without seeds

Mushrooms and toadstools belong to a group of plants called fungi. Fungi flourish in autumn because there is plenty of rain and it is not too cold. Above all there are plenty of dead leaves for them to grow on. Fungi get their food from dead and rotting plants.

Look at the underside of a mushroom. You will see lots of gills. These are where the spores are made. Spores are like seeds and the mushroom has many hundreds of them.

Project: Making spore patterns

You will need
- Some large mushrooms with the stalks cut off
- A sheet of white paper

What to do

1. Place the mushrooms with the gills down on the paper.

2. Leave them like this for several hours, then gently remove the mushrooms.

Can you see the patterns left behind? These are made by the spores that have fallen out of the gills.

WARNING: MANY FUNGI ARE POISONOUS. NEVER PICK THEM FROM THE WILD.

Right: Not all fungi simply drop their spores. Some, like the puffball, send them shooting into the air. There they fly away on the breeze to settle and grow elsewhere.

Did you know that yeast is a kind of fungus? Yeast is used to make bread. It produces a gas, which makes the bread rise. Yeast is also used in the making of beer and wine.

Project: Watching yeast at work

You will need
- A small plastic bag
- Sticky tape
- Some dried yeast
- Water
- A little sugar

What to do

1. Make up a mixture of yeast and water, following the directions on the packet. You may need to add sugar.

2. Pour the mixture into the plastic bag.

3. Seal the bag with the sticky tape to make sure that no air can get into it.

4. Put the bag in a warm room by a radiator.

What happens to the yeast mixture? What happens to the plastic bag?

Birds and flight

It is not only seeds and spores that fly away in autumn. Birds like swallows and martins fly great distances to warmer countries for the winter.

Birds, like this blue tit, are the masters of the air. Their bodies are specially designed for flight, with muscles that are very powerful for their size.

To fly well a bird must have a strong, but light skeleton. It must have large lungs to take in extra **oxygen** for the hard work of flying. And, of course, it must have wings with feathers.

There are two main sorts of feathers. The soft down feathers keep the birds warm by trapping air. The larger contour feathers have several uses. The most important contour feathers are those on the wings. These are called flight feathers.

Project: Make a feather helicopter

You will need
- Four long flight feathers
- A piece of dowel rod about 20cm long
- A cork with a hole through the middle
- Plasticine
- A stop watch
- A chair

What to do

1. Push the feathers into the cork around its edge, making sure that they are evenly spaced.

2. Push the dowel rod through the middle of the cork until about a centimetre shows at the top.

3. Twist the feathers so that they are at an angle to the cork, like the blades of a propeller.

4. Fix the ball of Plasticine to the long end of the dowel rod.

5. Stand on a chair and drop your helicopter. Measure the time it takes to reach the ground with your stopwatch.

You may need to adjust the angle of the feathers and the amount of Plasticine you use to make the helicopter work properly.

Looking at feathers

All birds have feathers, even those that don't fly. The central part of the feather is the shaft. Out of the shaft grow hundreds of **barbs**. These are locked together by millions of tiny hooks.

When all the wing feathers are overlapped they make a strong, flexible wing.

A flight feather

Shaft

Barbs

Hooks

Quill

Project: Looking at feathers

What to do

1. Take one of the feathers and run your finger down the barbs towards the quill. Can you separate the different barbs?

2. Run your finger back up towards the tip of the feather. What happens to the barbs you have separated?

3. Dip the feather in water. Take it out and shake it. Does it stay wet?

Left: Birds must take great care of their feathers. Removing dirt and dust is called preening.

4. Repeat these steps with the other wing feathers. Are they all the same?

5. Now repeat these steps with the downy feathers. What happens?

6. Examine a wing feather under a magnifying glass. Can you see the tiny rows of hooks along the barb?

Gliders

Birds flap their wings so that they can move around in the sky and to take off and land. Once they are in the air, some large birds use their wings to glide. Albatrosses can glide for days without ever flapping their wings.

You can make a glider of your own and test how far it can fly.

Project: Make a glider

You will need

- A long, thin tube of light plastic foam about 80cm long (the kind that is used to insulate water pipes)
- Three sheets balsa wood 0.3cm thick: one 10cm x 90cm, one 10cm x 30cm and one 10cm x 13cm
- Rubber bands
- Plasticine
- Two pieces of thin card each about 8cm x 3cm
- Glue
- Sandpaper

What to do

1. Round off the ends of the three pieces of balsa wood with the sandpaper.

2. Fix the long balsa wood sheet about a third of the way along the top of the foam tube using the rubber bands. This will form the wings.

3. Fix the second piece of balsa wood near the back of the tube at the bottom. This will form the tail.

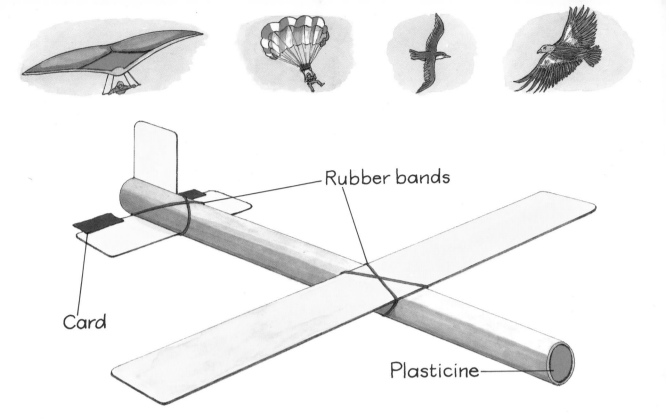

Rubber bands

Card

Plasticine

4. Slide the last piece of balsa wood into the slit in the tube. This will form the **rudder**.

5. Glue a piece of card to each back edge of the tail. These will help the glider to fly.

6. Hold the glider carefully by the wings. Add Plasticine to its nose until it balances.

7. Test your glider to see how far it can fly.

Real gliders are towed into the air by small aeroplanes and glide on updrafts of warm air.

The night sky

Autumn is a good time to look at the night sky. It gets dark earlier in the evening so you can look at the stars before you go to bed.

Astronomers can recognize the hundreds of stars by their position in the sky. These can change during the year. They also differ when seen from different parts of the Earth.

One of the best ways to identify stars is to find the ones that make up groups called **constellations**.

Look at the star charts on these pages. They show some of the constellations that you can see from the northern and southern parts of the Earth. Can you recognize any of these constellations in the night sky where you live?

A star tube will help you identify the constellations.

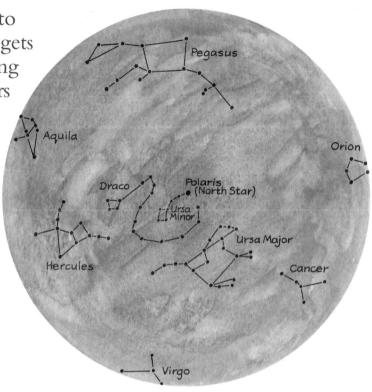

The northern sky.

Project: Making a star tube

You will need
- A large cardboard tube
- Some round pieces of black paper, each a little bigger than the end of the tube
- A white pencil
- Rubber bands
- A pin

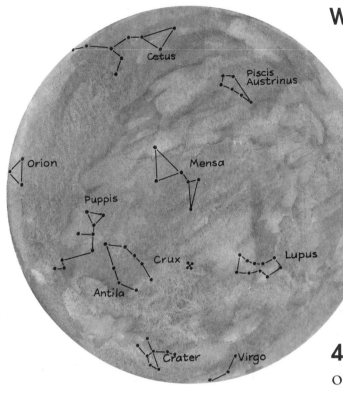

The southern sky.

Constellations labelled: Cetus, Piscis Austrinus, Orion, Mensa, Puppis, Crux, Lupus, Antila, Crater, Virgo

What to do

1. Draw a circle around the end of the tube on to a piece of black paper.

2. Make pin holes within this circle in the shape of one of the constellations.

3. Cut some slits around the edge of the big circle.

4. Fix the black paper circle over the end of the tube with a rubber band.

5. Look down the other end of your tube to see the stars.

6. Mark different constellations on the other pieces of paper.

Animals in autumn

Some animals use the autumn to prepare for their winter hibernation. Others prefer basking in the autumn sun.

The red admiral butterfly (below left) makes the most of the autumn sun, while the beetle (below) prefers damp shade.

Here are three experiments to see what kind of **environment** woodlice prefer.

Project: Observing woodlice

You will need
- 10 woodlice
- A deep tray
- A piece of black paper
- A table lamp
- Some damp sand

What to do

1. Cover half of the tray with the black paper and shine the light on to the other half.

2. Put the woodlice on to the tray. Watch how they move around.

3. Count the woodlice in each part of the tray every minute for 10 minutes.

4. Make a record of your count as a graph like this.

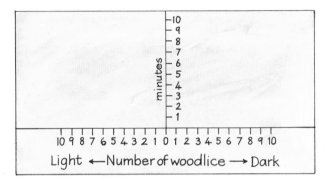

5. Now repeat this experiment, but this time place half of the tray near to a radiator and cover the whole tray with the black paper.

6. Remove the paper every minute for 10 minutes and record where the woodlice are.

7. Repeat steps 5 and 6, but this time fill half of the tray with damp sand.

8. Return the woodlice to the place where you found them.

Put all your results on to a chart like this:

Environment	Number of woodlice after 10 minutes
Light	
Dark	
Dry	

Which of these environments do the woodlice prefer? Which of these environments would you prefer?

REMEMBER TO TREAT THE WOODLICE WITH CARE. THEY ARE LIVING ANIMALS.

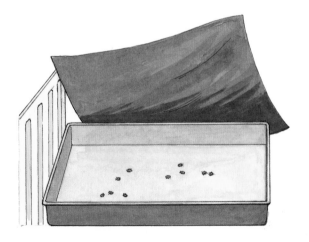

Notes for Teachers and Parents

What is autumn? (Pages 70-71)
The seasons are primarily controlled by two factors: the position of the Earth in its orbit around the Sun, and the inclination of the Earth's axis. When the northern and southern hemispheres are pointed towards the Sun, it is summer in the respective hemispheres. When the Sun is directly overhead the Equator it is autumn and spring. Other seasonal variations can be explained by the Sun's relative position to the Earth. In summer, the Sun is higher in the sky and the Sun's rays are concentrated in a small area. In winter, the rays hit that part of the Earth at an oblique angle and are more spread out. Autumn can be thought of as a transitional period between summer and winter.

Autumn fruits (Pages 72-73)
Fruits are the ripened ovary of a plant, in which the seeds are formed. Most fruits ripen following pollination of a flower. There are some fruits that develop normally, but, for some genetic reason, have no seeds. Bananas are an example of such a fruit. Trying to classify fruits can lead children into difficulty. A blackberry, for example, is not a berry at all, but a collection of little drupes. Many nuts are in fact drupe stones. The hazelnut and the sweet chestnut are true nuts, but the walnut and the almond are drupe stones. The rose hip, because it is formed from different parts of the flower is often not considered to be a true fruit at all. Common sense suggests that it should be drupe.
An important botanical differentiation is made between biologically dry fruits, such as the poppy capsule, and the pods of legumes and those fruits that remain succulent. Virtually all other fruits fall into this category.

Fruit stains (Pages 74-75)
The activities in this section are an example of a controlled fair test. All the conditions should remain constant — the amount of water and its temperature, the amount of powder, the amount of stirring and the stains themselves should be constant. The water need not be too hot. Nearly all the main brands of washing powder or washing liquid can be used within a wide variation of temperatures starting at 30°C. Care should be exercised if biological powders are used because some children may be allergic to them.

Fruit acidity (Pages 76-77)
This section introduces children to the elementary chemistry of some common substances. At this stage only acids are recognized, all other substances being non-acids. Children can later be introduced to the fact that the 'opposite' of an acid is an alkali. They will need to understand that strong alkalis are as unpleasant as acids, and therefore great care has to be taken when using them. Simple litmus paper, available from most good chemists, need only be used at this stage. Blue litmus paper will be turned red by all acids. There are other indicators that give different colours for different concentrations of acid or alkali. The best one to use to give a complete range of colours is universal indicator. This changes colour to a deep red for a strong acid (pH 0-1) to deep violet for a strong alkali (pH 13-14). The mid-point of the scale shows a change from yellow to green at pH 7. Indicators made from red cabbage and other plants will also give a wide range of colours. These will not, however, all be the same, so a comparison with a known indicator is essential before any conclusions can be drawn.

Seed dispersal (Pages 78-79)
Most children understand the planting of seeds. This section asks them to consider plant distribution from the starting point of seed dispersal. Although most plants, particularly the larger ones, only seed in the autumn, many, the dandelion for example, seed several times a year. The dandelion is well known for its form of seed dispersal. Other methods of dispersal include those employed by fruits such as the burdock, which have hooks that can catch on to an animal's fur (or a human's clothes). Many succulent fruits are eaten by animals and the seeds are subsequently dispersed in the animal's droppings. Many pod fruits split open when they dry, showering their seeds in all directions. Some tropical fruits like coconuts can be dispersed for many kilometres simply by falling into the sea. The work suggested with the well-known winged seeds will not only help children to understand this important process, but also introduce them to a more scientific approach to basic ecology.

Plants without seeds (Pages 80-81)
Fungi are a special group of plants. They have a simple structure, and are dependent upon the absorption of organic materials for their food. They have no chlorophyll, but in other regards are a plant. What we see of the fungi are the

reproductive structures, most of the remaining plant is inconspicuous. The well-known fungi are particularly visible during the early part of a wet and warm autumn. They produce thousands of spores, and have very efficient dispersal mechanisms. Fungi spores differ from seeds in that they have no embryo.

There are many thousands of different species of fungi, and yeast is one of the most simple forms. It is made up of a single cell, and reproduces by budding. Various forms have many industrial uses. These strains, all originating from the original wild yeast, *Saccharomyces cerevisiae*, include brewers' and bakers' yeast, as well as those used for the making of wine. During the fermentation process sugar is converted to alcohol, and carbon dioxide gas is produced. This is the gas that expands the plastic bag, and raises the bread.

Birds and flight (Pages 82-83)

It is very difficult to show children how birds use their wings to fly. It is probably best that they should see a video recording. Making the helicopter will at least give them hands-on experience of using the feathers in flight, albeit in a limited fashion. It is very important to make sure that the feathers are at the correct angle, or pitch. Children will have to experiment with this to make the helicopter spin.

Looking at feathers (Pages 84-85)

Many bird topics stop short at a study of the bird's anatomy. However, they are the only animals to be equipped with feathers, so a close look at these structures is valuable. The flight or contour feathers cover the body, and include the primaries, secondaries and the tail feathers. A typical flight feather has a central shaft, the rachis. The quill is the thick end of the shaft. Attached to this is the vane, or web, of barbs. When the barbs of the web are separated, minute hooks can just be seen. These are the barbules and on these are even smaller barbicels, which act like fasteners. In this way the web can be reformed when the bird is preening.

The down feathers are the fluffy feathers found on nestlings, but in many birds they persist through life. They keep the bird warm. A third very simple structure is the filo plume. These can usually be seen only when the other feathers have been removed.

Gliders (Pages 86-87)

The study of flight involves a knowledge of forces. Whatever propels the object forward is called thrust. The forward movement produces lift. This is brought about by the movement of air over the wings, so forming a partial vacuum. The air pressure is therefore higher on the underside of the wings forcing it upwards. This is the so-called 'Bernoulli principle': the faster the flow the lower the pressure. There are two more forces at work on any flying machine: drag, the opposite to thrust, is the friction on the machine caused by its passage through the air; and gravity, which will try to pull it down.

The technology of making gliders is simple, although there are some important things to note. You should be able to balance the glider by placing your finger tips under the ends of the wings. You can make the glider balance by a combination of weight in the nose, and the position of the wings along the body. Tail flaps (elevators) will make the glider go up or down, and when flat provide extra lift.

Children can experiment with different wing configurations, with the tail at the front and the wings at the back, for example.

The night sky (Pages 88-89)

Astronomy is a difficult subject to study at school because it is a night-time activity. However, children can make these simple star tubes during a topic about space. The technology needed to make them is basic, but tracing the constellations will introduce them to another aspect of the universe. Stars vary in magnitude (brightness) even within constellations. This can be shown by making a slightly bigger hole for the brighter stars.

Animals in autumn (Pages 90-91)

This section allows children to carry out some simple ecological and behavioural experiments. Most of the studies they make at this level are of the basic observational kind. This work will help children understand the habits of animals as well as their ecological needs. It will also help them understand science and experimentation.

The woodlouse is not an insect as its name seems to suggest, but a terrestrial crustacean — the same group that includes shrimps, crabs and lobsters. Choice chambers can be made out of two separate containers with only a small corridor between them. However, the tray suggested for this experiment is quite sufficient. Children should be taught to handle the creatures with care and respect, and not to subject them to extremes of heat or cold.

Further reading

Fitzgerald, Janet, *Autumn in the Wood*, (Science Through the Seasons), (Evans 1992)

Harlow, Rosie and Morgan, Gareth, *The Seasons*, (Fun With Science), (Kingfisher 1991)

Pluckrose, Henry, *Changing Seasons*, (Franklin Watts 1993)

Woolfit, Gabrielle, *Autumn*, (Science Through the Seasons), (Wayland 1995)

Association for Science Education, *Be Safe*, 2nd edition (1990)

Glossary

Antarctic The part of the world around the South Pole, where the land is always frozen and covered with snow.

Arctic The part of the world around the North Pole, where the sea is always frozen.

Barb The jagged vanes on a bird's feather.

Constellation A small group of stars that appear to stay the same distance from each other in the night sky. They are often given a name.

Environment The place where an animal or plant lives, and all the many things that affect its life.

Indicator In science this is a substance that changes colour when put into acids or alkalis.

Lines of latitude Imaginary lines drawn around the Earth.

Litmus An indicator made from a plant dye.

Oxygen The gas in the air that we and almost all other living things need to live and breathe.

Rudder The the tail of an aeroplane, or part of a boat, needed to steer the craft.

SCIENCE FUN THROUGH THE SEASONS

Winter

Science Projects

SCIENCE FUN THROUGH THE SEASONS

Winter

Science Projects

Notes on the National Curriculum

Now that Programmes of Study have been given a higher profile in the National Curriculum, teachers will be able to decide for themselves precisely where these activities fit into their topics. However, for help with assessment of the relevant levels, the activities shown in the book involve the following Attainment Targets:

Science
Teachers will find that the activities in this book coincide with many of the programmes of study in Key Stages 1 and 2. They will apply to the following Attainment Targets:-

Attainment Target 1: Experimental and investigative science All practical testing and experimentation that children undertake meet many of these requirements.

Attainment Target 2: Life processes and living things All the work involving the science of animals and plants meets many of the requirements of this Attainment Target. These not only include the life processes, but also adaptation, evolution and variation.

Attainment Target 3: Materials and their properties Much of the work involving temperature, ice and insulation meets the requirements of Key Stages 1 and 2.

Attainment Target 4: Physical processes The work on temperature, ice, insulation and the freezing of water also meets the requirements of this Attainment Target, as does the work on friction and the experiments with snow shoes.

Geography
Teachers will find many of the activities described in this book within the Programmes of Study for both Key Stages 1 and 2. Practical work involving maps, globes and the effects of weathering will be relevant to the section 'Geographical Skills'. Experiments involving wind chill, snow shoes and the general adaptation to the environment meet the requirements of the section 'Places'.

Technology
Many of the skills required to carry out the practical work in this book meet the design and making requirements for this document.

Teachers need to be aware of the opportunities to involve other areas of the curriculum - mathematics, languages and even art are other subjects involved in good primary science.

Contents

* Words in bold in the text are explained in the glossary.

What is winter?

There are four seasons – spring, summer, autumn and winter. Winter is the coldest season of the year. At the North and South Poles the winter is long, dark and very cold. It is not like this everywhere. In countries near the middle part of the world, winter may not be very different from summer.

Here are two signs that winter has come.
- The leaves have fallen from most of the trees.
- It's often cold or frosty in the morning.

Can you think of any more?

The trees in this picture have shed their leaves for the winter. What are trees that do this called?

PROJECT: Make a seasons zigzag book

The northern and southern parts of the world are called **hemispheres.** They have their winter at opposite times of the year. This zigzag book shows the seasons in each part.

You will need
- A length of card
- Felt tip pens

What to do

1. Fold the card into four equal parts, like a zigzag.

2. Think of some simple pictures, or symbols, for each season. Draw a symbol on each part of the book, in the right order, starting with winter.

3. Turn your card so the drawings are upside down, then turn it over, keeping them upside down.

4. Draw the symbols again, but this time start with summer.

5. Write the months for the seasons of the northern hemisphere on one side of the book. Write the months for the seasons of the southern hemisphere on the other side.

Even though the seasons are different, the months will be on the same page on each side of your book. Do you know which hemisphere your country is in?

103

Temperature

It's easy to tell if things are warm or cold by feeling them. Sometimes it's important to know exactly how warm or cold something is. For this we use an instrument called a thermometer. This measures temperature. When it is hot the temperature is high. When it is cold the temperature is low.

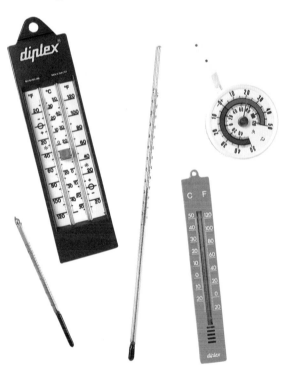

This picture shows some of the different kinds of thermometers that there are.

PROJECT: Make a thermometer

Temperature is measured in degrees. Not everybody uses the same measure. Some people use the **Fahrenheit scale**, some use the **Celsius scale**. You can make a cardboard thermometer showing both.

You will need
- Three pieces of card, two 21cm x 30cm (8in x 12in), one 15cm x 30cm (6in x 12in)
- Glue or stapler
- Felt tip pens
- A real thermometer
- Scissors

What to do

1. Cut a long thin slit in one large piece of card.

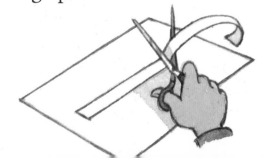

2. Glue or staple this piece of card to the other large piece of card along both long sides and one short side.

3. Colour the middle of the narrow piece of card red, and slide it between the other two pieces. The red colour will show through the slit.

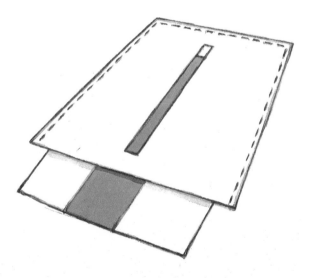

4. Copy the temperatures on this drawing on to your cardboard thermometer.

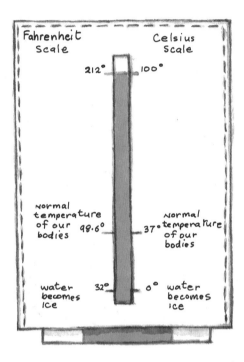

Fahrenheit Scale
Celsius Scale
212°   100°
Normal temperature of our bodies 98.6°   37° Normal temperature of our bodies
water becomes ice 32°   0° water becomes ice

Take the temperature outside every day for a week with a real thermometer. Record it on your cardboard thermometer. Compare it to the temperature of your classroom or bedroom.

NEVER TOUCH ANYTHING YOU THINK MAY BE VERY HOT OR VERY COLD.

Looking at ice

When it is cold outside, water freezes on ponds and puddles. These **experiments** show you what happens to water when it freezes.

PROJECT: A freezing experiment

You will need
- A clear plastic cup, half filled with water
- A marker pen

What to do

1. Put a mark on the cup at the level of the water.

2. Place the cup in the freezer, until the water is frozen.

3. Look at the level of the ice in the cup. Has the level risen or fallen? Do you think there is any more or less water in the cup now it is frozen?

4. Let the water melt again. Now where is the water level?

PROJECT: An iceberg experiment

Icebergs are huge masses of ice that float in the cold seas of the far north and far south. They can be a danger to ships. This project shows you why.

This iceberg is in the sea off the coast of Antarctica.

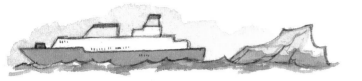

You will need

- Some ice cubes
- A deep tray of water
- A thermometer

What to do

1. Test the temperature of the water with a thermometer. Record it on a graph like the one on this page.

2. Float the ice cubes in the water. How much of the cube shows above the water? How much is under the water?

Much more of an iceberg is below the water than above it. This makes it a danger to ships.

3. Leave the ice cubes in the water until they disappear. Does the water feel colder or hotter as the ice cubes get smaller? Take the temperature of the water every 15 minutes as the ice melts.

4. Plot the temperature readings on your graph.

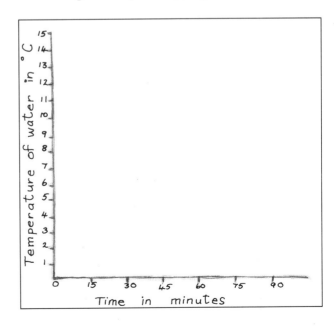

107

Melting ice

Local and city councils spread salt on roads in the winter. This project will explain why they do this.

This lorry is spreading salt on icy roads. It has big wheels to help stop it skidding on the slippery ice and snow.

PROJECT: Ice and salt

> ### You will need
> - An ice cube
> - Some salt

What to do

1. Sprinkle some salt on to a freshly frozen ice cube.

2. Describe what happens to the ice. Can you hear anything when the salt mixes with the ice?

It is more difficult for salty water to freeze, than for fresh water. It needs a lower temperature to turn into ice. This means it takes longer to freeze.

PROJECT: Another melting experiment

You will need

- A large block of ice (you can make one by freezing water in a plastic ice cream box)
- A piece of string or wire
- Two 0.5kg (1lb) weights
- A shallow tray

What to do

1. Put your ice block on the tray. Wear gloves if you need to touch the ice.

2. Tie a weight to each end of the string or wire.

3. Put the piece of string or wire over the ice block so that it stretches tightly over the middle of the block. If your string or wire is very long, you can stand the tray on a box so the weights can hang freely.

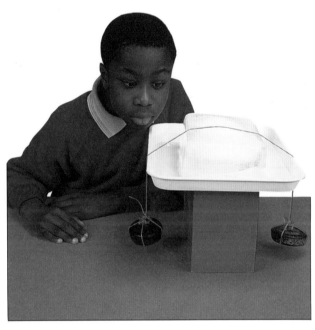

4. What is happening to the wire or string? Look carefully at the ice. What is happening to the top of the block?

Try putting your ice block in the freezer. Does the same thing happen?

Weathering

You have already seen that water takes up more space when it freezes. Water collects in the cracks of rocks. When it freezes it breaks the rock open. Wind and rain wear the rocks away too, but freezing will break them up first. This process is called weathering.

The small rocks have been broken off the mountain by ice.

Here are some experiments to show how ice breaks up rocks and soil.

PROJECT: Freezing and weathering

You will need
- Some soft rocks. Chalk is the best rock for this test, but if you can't get it, bits of broken house brick can be used instead.
- A shallow tray

What to do

1. Soak your rocks in water for two days.

2. Put them in the freezer, on the tray.

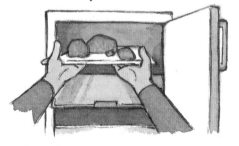

What happens to the rock when the water freezes?

PROJECT: Frozen soil

Gardeners and farmers like the soil to be broken into small pieces. They dig or plough the soil in autumn, so that winter frosts can break up the lumps.

You will need
- Some clay from the garden, or try potters' clay
- A deep plastic tray

What to do

1. Put some wet clay in the tray.

2. Smooth it down carefully.

3. Put the tray in the freezer. Leave it at least a day.

How hard is the frozen clay?

4. Let the ice melt and see what difference it makes to the clay.

Keeping warm

We all need to keep warm in cold weather. We wear warm clothes. Birds fluff up their feathers and trap warm air under them. Some animals have extra layers of fat, or grow thicker fur.

This blue tit looks fat because it has fluffed out its feathers to help it keep warm.

We need to keep our houses warm. We light the fire or turn on the central heating. We put materials in the loft to stop the warm air getting out. These act as **insulators**.

PROJECT: An insulation experiment

Some materials are better at insulating than others. The next experiment shows us how to find out which materials are the best.

ASK AN ADULT TO HELP WITH THIS EXPERIMENT.

You will need
- Several tins, all the same size
- A box for each tin, all the same size
- A thermometer for each tin
- Kitchen foil
- Hot water
- Different materials. Try a woollen jumper or scarf, newspaper, sawdust, straw, or polystyrene chips.
What other things can you think of?

What to do

1. Put a tin into each box.

2. Pack a different material round each tin, leaving one with nothing around it.

3. Fill all the tins with hot water.

4. Make a lid for every tin out of kitchen foil.

5. Measure the temperature of each tin every five minutes for half an hour with your thermometers.

Write down your results on a chart like this one.

Time in minutes	Temperature in °C				
	Tin 1	Tin 2	Tin 3	Tin 4	Tin 5
start 0					
5					
10					
15					
20					
25					
30					

Which material is the best insulator?
Why did we keep one tin with nothing round it?
Insulating materials have many uses. Look around your home or school and see how many you can find.

Wind chill

We can keep warm by wearing extra clothes. When there is a cold wind, these may not be enough to protect you from **wind chill**. Here is an experiment to find out what happens to the temperature if the wind is blowing.

PROJECT: Measuring wind chill

You will need
- A large piece of paper
- A pencil
- A thermometer

What to do

1. Draw a plan of your school grounds, garden or local park like the one at the bottom of this page.

2. Mark on it about ten places that are sheltered, but not under cover, for example, behind a bush or a tree.

3. Go outside when the wind is blowing. Measure the temperature in these sheltered places.

You could measure just twice. Once in the middle of the playground, garden or park, and once against the side of a building. How might having only two lots of information, instead of ten, affect your results? Apart from being sheltered, can you think of other reasons why it might be warmer against the side of a building?

4. Take the temperatures again, standing as near to the sheltered places as you can, but this time in the wind. Are there any differences?

Clothes that protect you from wind chill need not be thick, as long as the wind cannot blow through them. Skiing clothes are a good example of this.

5. Write down your results like this.

place	Temperature in °C	
	out of wind	in wind
1. Behind tree		
2. Near bush		
3.		

In an experiment like this the number of measurements is important.

Slipping and sliding

Above: This boy's ice skates are designed to slide easily on the ice. How are they different from ordinary shoes?

It is difficult to walk on ice as it is very smooth and you may slip, although it can be fun to slide or skate on it.

PROJECT: Testing shoes for grip

When we are just walking about, we don't want to slip and slide. Some shoes have ridges or patterns on the soles to stop us sliding. Others don't. Look at your own, and your friends' or family's shoes. Find out who is most likely to slip over!

What to do

1. Put the weight inside a shoe.

2. Place the shoe on a smooth floor.

3. Hook the spring balance on to the top of the shoe.

4. Hold the spring balance, and use it to pull the shoe along the floor.

How hard did you have to pull? The number shown on the scale of the spring balance is your measurement of pull. The higher this number is, the less likely you are to slip over in those shoes. Do this for all the shoes and write down your results.

type of shoe	measurement of pull		
	with shoe on the floor	with shoe on the carpet	with shoe on a sanded board
trainer			
wellington boot			

5. Now, try doing the same experiment on different surfaces. Try carpet or a sanded board. Compare your results with your first set.

When there is ice on roads and pavements, local and city councils often put down sand or grit. Why do you think this is? What could they mix with it to make it work even better?

Snow shoes

Have you ever tried walking in deep snow? Imagine what it would be like walking through a snow drift that reached up to your waist!

The Cree Indians live in a part of North America where the land is often covered in deep snow. They wear special shoes, made of wood and strips of animal skin. This experiment will show you how these snow shoes work.

PROJECT: Make some snow shoes

You will need
- Matchsticks or cocktail sticks
- Plasticine
- Two pieces of thick card, each about 2cm x 2cm (1in x 1in)
- Glue
- Some soft snow or very wet sand in a tray
- Scales and weights

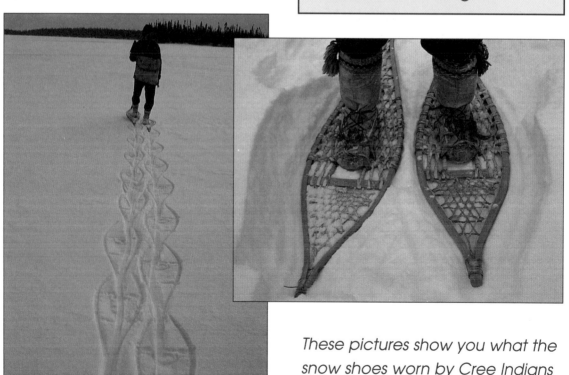

These pictures show you what the snow shoes worn by Cree Indians look like.

118

What to do

If you are using snow, do this experiment outside, or only bring it in when you are ready to use it.

1. Divide the plasticine into two large balls weighing about 60g (2oz) and two smaller balls weighing about 15g (0.5oz).

2. Make two model people, using matchsticks for legs and arms.

3. Glue the two small squares of card to the feet of one of the models. You may need to use a little more plasticine to help the card stick.

4. Weigh the models again to check they weigh the same. Add plasticine to one if is it lighter.

5. Lower them both gently on to the snow or wet sand. What happens to the model without the card shoes?

This polar bear has very wide feet which help stop it sinking into the snow.

Plants

Most plants stop growing in the winter. Soft leaves and stems that grew in summer die and fall off. Water, which plants need to grow, is often frozen solid. When it freezes, the water inside plants turns to ice too. What would happen to a plant with a lot of water in its leaves and stems? Try this experiment in your freezer.

PROJECT: Freezing plants

You will need
- Two raw potatoes
- A bowl
- A knife

What to do

1. Put one potato into the freezer for at least a day.

2. Take it out of the freezer and put it into the bowl. Let it **thaw** out.

3. Compare your thawed potato with the one that has not been frozen.

Try cutting them both in half.

ASK AN ADULT TO HELP WITH THIS EXPERIMENT.

Water in plants is held in small units called **cells**. When the water freezes it gets bigger and breaks the soft walls of these cells.

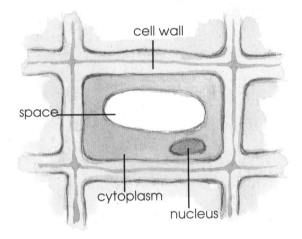

This is a simplified drawing of a plant cell. Cytoplasm is mostly made of water which keeps the plant alive.

Some trees and plants are protected from cold winters. Look at the leaves of a pine tree or a holly tree which stay green all winter. Is it easy or difficult to break or tear them? Why do you think they are shiny? Do the last experiment again with a handful of pine needles or holly leaves, and some soft leaves. Get permission to use one or two soft leaves from an indoor plant if there are none outside. This time put them into plastic bags before putting them into the freezer. Compare your bags of leaves after they have thawed.

Pine trees can be covered in snow for many weeks in winter.

Animals

Wild animals find it difficult to get enough food in winter. The days are short, plants do not grow, and the ground may be covered in snow. The way that their bodies use up, or digest, food makes them warm. Thick fur or hair keeps the warmth in.

Animals survive in different ways. Some, like this squirrel, make stores of food which they dig up when they are hungry.

Some birds and animals, like these caribou, move to warmer places for the winter. This is called migration.

Some animals, like this dormouse, sleep during winter. This is called hibernation.

Tiny animals have problems, because they get cold much quicker than larger animals.

This shrew has to keep eating for most of the day to keep warm. A day's food can weigh four times its own weight. It is so small that it will get cold very quickly if it does not eat all this food, and could die.

PROJECT: Food and warmth

You will need
- Two tins, one large and one very small
- Hot water
- Kitchen foil

In this experiment you have to imagine that the hot water is the tin's food!

What to do

1. Fill the tins with hot water.

2. Make a lid for each tin from kitchen foil.

3. Feel the tins with your hands every five minutes.

Which tin gets cold first? Imagine the coldness means all the tin's food is used up. You would have to refill it with hot water to keep it warm. This what the shrew has to do.

ASK AN ADULT TO HELP WITH THIS EXPERIMENT.

Notes for Teachers and Parents

Day length (Pages 102–103)

This topic is not included in the main text because of the difficulties for children in obtaining precise measurements, although they will know by direct observation that day length is shorter in winter. However, control technology, using a light sensitive cell in conjunction with a suitable computer program, can be utilised to provide these measurements. The problem of continuous computer use for schools can be overcome by running the program at weekends, or even during the winter holiday. Children can also be made aware of the different day lengths, and the winter and summer months of both hemispheres, by the use of a globe. If a torch, representing the sun, is shone onto the globe, the resulting shadows will help show children the differences between the seasons, and, if the globe is spun, day and night as well.

Temperature (Pages 104–105)

Perhaps we notice temperature more often in winter than any other time of the year. The extremes of coldness and warmth seem more obvious to us, whether it is through the necessity of wearing extra clothes or checking the level of the central heating. Making a thermometer will help children understand specific temperatures in the natural world. While they will already know the difference between hot and cold, they will not have experience of a range of temperature, their own body heat compared to the temperature of a warm bath, or just how cold it has to be for water to freeze. It is important that they should understand that a thermometer is just another measuring instrument. There is nothing magical about it. A thermometer measures degrees of temperature, just as a ruler measures centimetres or inches, or a clock measures time.

Water and ice (Pages 106–109)

Most substances can exist as liquids, solids, or gases, or even as materials somewhere between these three states. However, water is the only one that children can easily experience in all three states. Water is at its most dense at $4°C$, but freezes solid at $0°C$. Most other substances are at their greatest density when solid. Water is different in that, when it freezes, its molecules reform into a lightweight lattice, and hence it will float. Children should not be expected to understand this in detail, but they might ask questions which will need some scientific answer.

The various experiments with ice in this section are designed to give children experience of experimental skills, such as observation and hypothesizing. History records that Michael Faraday carried out a similar series of experiments, although he would have understood less than we do about the nature and behaviour of ice. When we float ice in water, the ice takes heat from the water. Eventually, equilibrium is reached when the ice has melted, and we have a dish of cold water. When we add salt to snow or ice, the salt dissolves in the surface layer of moisture, releasing heat which melts the rest of the ice. The experiment with the large block of ice shows how the friction of the wire will generate heat, and so, temporarily at least, melt the ice. A similar process goes on between the blades of ice-skates and the surface of the ice.

Weathering (Pages 110–111)

Ice can affect the shape of the land in two ways. As great sheets of ice, or as large glaciers, it can carve out valleys and mountains. Even the hardest rocks can be ground down and re-shaped by the forces exerted by moving ice. Although less dramatic, but in the long run just as effective and more widespread, ice will shape the landscape in the form of frost. The experiments in this section will help children understand the force exerted by the ice as it expands, breaking up rocks and soil, as well as affecting roads and buildings in a similar manner.

This is a good opportunity for children to understand the problems of frozen water pipes, and also car radiators. They can learn that water pipes need to be covered with a suitable material, to stop the water freezing. They will understand that this cannot be done to a car radiator, but may know that anti-freeze is mixed with the water, which affects the temperature at which it freezes.

Keeping warm (Pages 112–113)

Various materials make good insulators, in that they do not conduct the heat away. Children should be encouraged to experiment with a range of materials, even if some of them are not apparently suitable. They could try water itself as an insulator. This set of experiments is valuable for showing what a 'fair test' means. Variables can easily be excluded, and one tin left with no insulation as a control, so that it can be seen that the tin itself does not provide the protection.

Wind chill (Pages 114-115)

This section allows the children to see the effects of a cold wind on the temperature. Research has shown us that we are much more likely to suffer the effects of exposure if we are wet and left unprotected from cold wind. You can extend the experiment and simulate the effect of wet clothes by placing a small piece of wet tissue or cloth over the bulb of the thermometer. When we are wet we lose heat quickly for two reasons. Water is a better conductor of heat than air, so if we have wet clothes and skin, heat is conducted away from our bodies more quickly than if we were dry. Secondly, the very process by which our wet clothes and skin dry out, evaporation, itself takes heat away from the body. It is important to take as many different readings as possible. This will not only allow for the possibility of experimental error, but will also show if the difference in the strength of the wind has any effect on the temperature. It will also help to give a range of more accurate readings in the sheltered areas. We do not want the readings to be altered by the warmth from the building. The structure of the building itself can be a reservoir of warm air, and even warm air from an open door can affect the temperature. If we can avoid these variables, we will have a truer picture of what happens in nature. Animals trap a layer of air under their fur or feathers which is warmed by their own body heat. Children need to be made aware that modern cold weather clothing is designed to do the same thing.

Slipping and sliding (Pages 116-117)

Friction is a force. Forces are pushes and pulls, and friction tends to pull objects away from the normal direction that they wish to follow. We often want to reduce friction, for instance we put oil into a car engine to reduce the wear and tear of constant friction. Walking on ice is an example of where increased friction is an advantage. With normal walking we rely on friction to allow us to push ourselves forward. Children can carry out experiments with different footwear on various surfaces from shiny to very rough to see which combinations give the best results. They might like to consider the implications of this in relation to tap dancing and running shoes.

Snow shoes (Pages 118-119)

This experiment shows the relationship between weight, surface area and pressure. It is very important that both the models are the same weight so that the effects of the card can be clearly seen. Where there are permanent environmental extremes, such as desert, extremes of temperature, or continuous snow and ice, people have to adapt their lives to these conditions. Wearing snow shoes is one such adaptation. Wearing special clothes or eating a particular diet are other ways by which people live in such conditions. We have seen in the sections on temperature and on wind chill how humans can deal with these extremes. Animals and plants have had to evolve, over many years, mechanisms to allow them to survive. These themes are expanded upon in the next two sections.

Plants (Pages 120-121)

Plants protect themselves in winter in various ways. Some pass the winter as seeds, while other, larger plants shed their leaves and remain dormant. Some have evolved as evergreens and have leaves with a protective coating of wax, although even evergreens will remain dormant during a cold winter, especially if the soil water remains frozen. Plants that have not evolved these mechanisms would not survive a cold winter. When a green plant is affected by frost, the water in the plant freezes, and by expanding breaks the cell wall. It is difficult to explain this to young children. They will see the effect of the frost - a brown, wilted plant. They cannot see the damage inside the plant. One possible way to explain this process is to fill a small plastic bag with water, tie it tightly, making sure there is no free air in the bag, and let the children feel it. It will be firm but still pliable, and can represent some of the softer kinds of plant cell (most plant cells have rigid walls). Put the bag into the freezer, freeze and then allow it to thaw. Hopefully the bag will have burst under the pressure of the ice, and the children can more easily imagine the effect this would have on a plant.

Animals (Pages 122-123)

Animals have even more ways of surviving winter than plants. We have already seen how they can protect themselves from the cold, although it is often the shortage of food and water that causes problems. The experiment in this section shows how animals which have a large surface area in comparison to their volume will quickly lose heat energy. Some animals have evolved metabolic systems which allow them to go without food for several weeks, or to store food and water in their bodies in the form of fat. Some migrate, some hibernate. Children need to understand that hibernation is not just 'going to sleep for the winter'. Few warm blooded animals truly hibernate. The process is even now not fully understood, although it involves the slowing down of all body processes, so that very little energy is required to stay alive. Hibernation is thought to be brought about by day length as much as temperature, although in cold blooded animals temperature does have a more direct effect.

Further reading

Fitzgerald, Janet, *Science through the seasons: Winter on the Farm* (Evans, 1989)

Fitzgerald, Janet, *Science through the seasons: Winter in the Wood* (Evans, 1987)

Williams, John, *Starting Technology: Air* (Wayland, 1990)

Williams, John, *Starting Technology: Time* (Wayland, 1990)

Association for Science Education *Be Safe*, 2nd edition (1990)

Glossary

Cell A tiny part of a plant or animal. Even a very small plant or animal can be made up of millions of cells.

Celsius scale A way of measuring temperature, named after Anders Celsius, which has 0° as the freezing point of water, and 100° as its boiling point.

Experiment A test made to discover something that is not known.

Fahrenheit scale A way of measuring temperature, which has 32° as the freezing point of water, and 212° as its boiling point.

Hemisphere A half of a ball (or sphere). The world is a sphere, and is divided into northern and southern halves, or eastern and western halves. Each half is called a hemi-sphere.

Insulator A material that can stop heat or electricity getting through. Most things that are not metal are good insulators.

Thaw To raise the temperature of something, usually ice, so that it melts.

Wind chill The extra coldness caused by the wind, often when blowing on wet clothes or skin.

Notes on the National Curriculum

Now that Programmes of Study have been given a higher profile in the National Curriculum, teachers will be able to decide for themselves precisely where these activities fit into their topics. However, for help with assessment of the relevant levels, the activities shown in the book involve the following Attainment Targets:

Science
Teachers will find that the activities in this book coincide with many of the programmes of study in Key Stages 1 and 2. They will apply to the following Attainment Targets:

Attainment Target 1: Experimental and investigative science All practical testing and experimentation that children undertake meet many of these requirements.

Attainment Target 2: Life processes and living things All the work involving the science of animals and plants meets many of the requirements of this Attainment Target. These not only include the life processes, but also adaptation, evolution and variation.

Attainment Target 3: Materials and their properties Much of the work involving temperature, structures and building materials, both natural and man-made, meets the requirements of Key Stages 1 and 2.

Attainment Target 4: Physical processes The work on temperature and its effects, as well as the work on kites and levers, meets the requirements of this Attainment Target.

Geography
Teachers will find many of the activities described in this book within the Programmes of Study for both Key Stages 1 and 2. Practical work involving wind direction and strength, and temperature and the greenhouse effect, will be relevant to the section *Geographical Skills*.

Technology
Many of the skills required to carry out the practical work in this book meet the design and making requirements for this document.

Teachers need to be aware of the opportunities to involve other areas of the curriculum — mathematics, languages and even art are other subjects involved in good primary science.

SCIENCE FUN THROUGH THE SEASONS

Spring
Science Projects

JOHN WILLIAMS

Evans

Evans Brothers Limited